FICTIONS OF FEMININE DESIRE

FICTIONS OF FEMININE DESIRE

Disclosures of Heloise

Peggy Kamuf

UNIVERSITY OF NEBRASKA PRESS
Lincoln and London

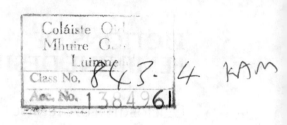
First Bison Book printing: 1987
Most recent printing indicated by the first digit below:
1   2   3   4   5   6   7   8   9   10

Library of Congress Cataloging in Publication Data
Kamuf, Peggy, 1947–
    Fictions of feminine desire.
    Bibliography: p. 163
    Includes index.
    1. French fiction—17th century—History and criti-
cism. 2. French fiction—18th century—History and
criticism. 3. Heloïse, 1101–1164. 4. Desire in lit-
erature. I. Title.
PQ645.K3   843'.4'09353   81-10290
ISBN 0-8032-2705-1   AACR2
ISBN 0-8032-7766-0 (pbk.)

FOR J.

CONTENTS

ACKNOWLEDGMENTS

During the two years spent on this project, I received support in many forms and from many sources. A grant from the American Council of Learned Societies funded an indispensable leave from teaching for a year. I am also grateful for financial support from the Research Committee and the College of Arts and Science at Miami University.

More difficult to calculate is my debt to the many friends, colleagues, and students who have not felt too imposed upon. Phil Lewis, Ron Rosbottom, and Paul de Man were generous with their support of this project in its earliest stages. My thanks to Nat Wing, English Showalter, Nancy K. Miller, Mitchell Greenberg, and Marie-Claire Vallois for their careful observations on various parts of the manuscript, and to my students, particularly Vivian Eeman, who were most patient while I tried out ideas on them. I am particularly glad to have had the benefit of Betsy Wing's perceptive readings.

I owe a much more general—finally unfathomable—debt to my two most knowing readers: Jane Gallop, without whom I have no doubt I could not have weathered the several crises that each chapter posed, and Jim Creech, the other in my life towards whom I was always writing.

INTRODUCTION
Prologue to What Remains

What is a crypt? No crypt presents itself. The grounds are so
disposed as to disguise and to hide: something, always a body in
some way. But also to disguise the act of hiding and to hide the
disguise: the crypt hides as it holds. Carved out of nature, some-
times making use of probability of facts, these grounds are not
natural. A crypt is never natural through and through, and if, as is
well known, *physis* has a tendency to encrypt (itself), that is
because it overflows its own bounds and encloses, naturally, its
others, all others. The crypt is thus not a natural place, but the
striking history of an artifice, an *architecture*, an artifact: of a place
comprehended within another but rigorously separate from it,
isolated from general space by partitions, an enclosure, an enclave.

Jacques Derrida, "Fors"

 I HAVE chosen as a point of entry into a certain body
of seventeenth and eighteenth-century fiction the
epilogue to Heloise's legendary passion for Abelard.
This review of the excess of woman's passion, which
is both ours and someone else's, begins, then, with the history of
a curious survival, the reading of a bodily residue.

Peter Abelard died on April 21, 1142, at the Abbey of Cluny.
His body was clandestinely transferred several months later for
burial at the Paraclete, the monastery he had founded and that
Heloise administered until her own death on May 16, 1164. She
was buried beside Abelard, probably in the same crypt. In 1497,
their remains were removed from the marshy site of this crypt in
a small chapel to separate tombs on either side of the choir in the
main sanctuary of the monastery. This transfer seems to have
been motivated by the concern to situate the tombs in a less
humid environment. The next exhumation and transfer, which
took place in 1621 and which once again placed the coffins in the
same crypt (this time before the main altar), probably had a quite
different motivation. Charlotte Charrier, whose careful research
I am merely summarizing here, suggests that the nuns at the

Paraclete were responding to a public curiosity about the lovers which the publication of their letters in 1616 had provoked.[1] This curiosity would later become a vogue and the convent a place of pilgrimage *pour les coeurs tendres* where, it seems, the nuns were eager to accommodate worldly interests. Contrary to monastic custom, these sentimental pilgrims were given access to the sanctuary to see the burial place. In 1768, the tombs were again opened and their contents verified by two physicians. A few years later, in 1780, another transfer took place. The bones were moved to the two halves of a single lead coffin which was set in a tomb before the altar. A witness at this exhumation noted that Abelard's skeleton was badly disintegrated while Heloise's had been pillaged of one of its teeth. Several epitaphs and statues were produced to embellish the new rearrangement of the remains, and visits to the Paraclete became more numerous than ever.

The prosperity of the monastery ended with the Revolution. The Paraclete was ravaged and finally put up for auction. The civil authorities intervened at this point to save the relics of the famous lovers with the result that in 1792 another exhumation and transfer was ordered from the demolished monastery to a chapel in the church at Nogent-sur-Seine. Once again, the coffin was opened, its contents examined, and, according to one participant at the ceremony, huge sums were offered for a single one of Heloise's teeth. Some time between this transfer and the next, in 1800, the new tomb was vandalized.

When the bones of Heloise and Abelard were next disinterred, it was at the insistence of the founder of the Musée des Monuments Français, Alexandre Lenoir, an art historian and archaeologist who had won a certain favor with General Bonaparte. As before, the coffin was opened and the skeletal contents catalogued. The unsealed coffin was in Lenoir's personal possession for several years, after its removal from Nogent-sur-Seine to his residence in Paris. It would appear from a number of contemporary accounts that during this time Lenoir freely extracted sentimental souvenirs from his treasure for distribution among his friends, mostly women. By 1807, the "remains" (the word was by then even more appropriate) had become once again pretext for a pilgrimage, but romantic Parisians now had to travel no further than the rue des Petits-Augustins, where Lenoir had finally opened his museum. The debris of Abelard and Heloise had been placed in an elaborate stone sarcophagus, itself contained in a funeral chapel situated in the museum's garden courtyard, which Lenoir named the Elysée. The chapel, which the museum's founder claimed was built from the rescued fragments of the cloister at the Paraclete, was in fact a *bricolage* of sculptural and architectural pieces from different periods and places. Statues and inscriptions had proliferated by this time, and the whole created a fantastic effect on the avid public. But the Elysée was not to be the final "resting" place either. A royal order of 1816 appropriated the buildings of Lenoir's museum and he had to find a new home for his monuments. The coveted bones were taken out of the sarcophagus, placed again in separate coffins, and solemnly transferred to Père-Lachaise cemetery. While the removal was accomplished with all the requisite religious and civil ceremony, there was no catalogue made of the remains at this point, an oversight which Charrier thinks may have been deliberate. Finally, after six months, Lenoir's fantastic mausoleum was reassembled at Père-Lachaise and, on November 6, 1817, what was left of Heloise's and Abelard's mortal relics was replaced in a tomb. It is still there, covered now with hearts intertwined around initials, the graffiti of several generations of love's pilgrims.

To the question, then, of what remains of Heloise's singular passion for Abelard, one answer might be this monument to an anachronistic romanticism. Clearly, the series of transfers to another site and the wholesale borrowings of souvenirs have left little intact with which to reconstruct a certain presence. As for the other relic of Heloise, a written corpus, it has undergone many more transformations than her carnal remnants. What one can read today in order to re-member Heloise—to put back together her various parts—is, therefore, as dubiously authentic as the tomb at Père-Lachaise. All that survives for sure is the process of *translation*, that is, both "the removal of remains from one place to another" and the "turning from one language into another" (*OED*). The name "Heloise"—in the epitaph on a grave, in the address of a letter—designates with certainty only this scattering and recuperation, uncovering and reburial of a remainder. In this process, no last word, no final resting place which does not leave something still to be said and exhumed. "Heloise," thus, names both our desire to retrieve what is lost in translation, to construct a more complete monument to the remains, and the inevitable persistence, all the same, of that construction's excess.

It will not be literary history in the ordinary sense that interests me here. Rather, the opening question—what remains of Heloise?—is one to which my answers are potentially irrelevant, maybe even impertinent, if seen from the point of view of established procedures of literary historical research. First of all, I make no contribution here to the debate over the historical authenticity of the letters of Heloise and Abelard.[2] Neither do I want to suggest necessarily that the authors of four seventeenth- and eighteenth-century texts wrote with a particular reference to this correspondence that can be retrieved. On the contrary, the possibility of such a retracing of an inheritance back to its source is explicitly put into question, particularly in the final two chapters of this book.

On the other hand, it is not literary history as such which is set aside here—certainly a vain project—but rather the practice of reading one text as descending from another along a straight line of authorial intention. While one might suppose, for example, that Rousseau had read a contemporary edition of the twelfth-century letters before writing *Julie, or the New Heloise*, nonetheless this novel cannot be confined within the reference of its title. Yet, I will also propose that it is the persistence of a certain Heloise in the novel that we have learned to overlook. Thus, I am suggesting both that the history of Heloise and Abelard is not a model for these later texts, all of which were written sometime after their history had been in vogue, and that something remains, nevertheless, from one work to the next as a souvenir of Heloise's persevering desire for Abelard. What I have set out to write, then, are some of the chapters in this other "history," the residue of a woman's excessive desire.

This history begins with a reading of Heloise's and Abelard's correspondence for several reasons, one of which we have already mentioned: the immense popularity of the medieval letters beginning in the late seventeenth-century but intensifying through the next century, when free "translations" proliferated at a remarkable rate. Thus, the period from 1669, when *The Portuguese Letters* first appeared, to 1782, the year *Les Liaisons Dangereuses* was published, was also marked by these other literary productions, now almost all considered of interest only as examples of a fad. To this historical coincidence, we add another: that of the twelfth-century letters with the major shift in literary and social perspective signaled by the predominance of the courtly love topos in medieval poetry.

Paul Zumthor, in an essay which was later reworked as an introduction to his translation of the correspondence, describes the courtly topos and rhetoric as making a space in the rational order for what had always been excluded: the heterosexual relation.

> Medieval man enclosed all that existed in rational and theoretical frames. Whatever did not fit into one of these frames was deemed not to exist, not to have cultural value, and to remain a barbarity which was repulsive to the mind. The passions of love remained at the margin of the conceptual universe, and therefore all the more tenacious—unconquered, deprived of both language and of that relative security which results from insertion in an order. We know that the Southern poets at the end of the eleventh century managed to overcome this inertia. They created, in a patchwork fashion, the rational frame that love needed in order finally to assert itself as a cultural value. This frame was the courtly topos and rhetoric. Thanks to them, the relation between the sexes ceased to be either a simple, biological function or a spiritual disorder. It took its place among other realities, in the series of rationally valid existences which were therefore aesthetically beautiful.[3]

Zumthor proceeds to read the letters of Heloise and Abelard at the juncture where "the verbal and imaginary world of the troubadours coincides, thanks to the chance of these extraordinary lives, with experience."[4] But that coincidence is one which in Zumthor's judgment can only result in a disillusionment, since "if [the courtly schema] satisfied the needs of expression and of worldly customs, it could not really resolve the conflicts of existence nor soothe a deep sorrow."[5] In other words, that insertion into the rational order which the courtly topos accomplishes still leaves the heterosexual relation painfully unable to settle its accounts.

To the extent that critics like the one cited above are correct in evaluating the emergence of courtly rhetoric as the first expression of sexual passion within accepted, rational categories, then in the letters which Heloise and Abelard exchanged (and which coincided with this "event") may very possibly reside a narration of the rational, logocentric reduction of sexual difference that has been a consistent legacy of our culture.[6] From this possibility there derives another: by reading the account as articulated by the rational structures of appropriation, one may still retrieve whatever exceeds these closed, specular circuits, what had to be excluded as "barbarous" and "repulsive." There, at the beveled margins of a culture's self-representation, where the reflection goes awry, one may glimpse perhaps a version of Heloise which was not serialized by the civilizing frames of her contemporaries nor yet by those of future generations.

If such an excavation of Heloise's crypt were able to bring to the surface even the slightest trace of the flesh which once encased her coveted bones, would it not then be possible to imagine another line of descent, another disposition of the remains? At the juncture of her woman's difference with the uniform values of an expanding culture, Heloise left an ambiguous double legacy. Besides the central exploitation of the Heloise story in the seventeenth and eighteenth centuries, which relied on their own mirrors to interpret the terms of the legacy, another, unauthorized, reading of the will was perhaps taking place. In the four succeeding chapters, I will try to put together some of the pieces of this scattered estate.

My principal focus in each of these chapters is on the particular structure which is working to appropriate and disguise the force of a woman's passion. In a first moment—that of *The Portuguese Letters*—the structure can be located in the subject / object syntax of the remembered discourse of seduction. The course which Mariana follows in the five letters is one which writes this syntax differently—and in a manner which exposes her desire to itself. With *The Princess de Clèves*, the sentence that operates to obscure the heroine's desire is not spoken in the lovers' exchange but in the exchange between mother and daughter, from where it can continue to echo and drown other voices. For the princess, then, extricating her own desire from this sentence cannot be a matter of reversing its syntax but would require a break in the closed dialogue with the parent. In *Julie, or the New Heloise*, it is a parent's name—the father's—which functions to suppress the woman's dissident passion and to bury the evidence of a difference within a singular identity. Finally, with *Les Liaisons Dangereuses*, we return to the syntax of seduction but as already doubled from the outset and therefore already reversed and uncovered. In this narrative of multiple seductions and multiple desires, the only space left for the appropriation of a disruptive difference is at the juncture of the fictional text with the text of the reader's reading. It is here as well that I conclude this book, and it will remain to my reader to assume—or not—the difference which no text can annihilate without leaving traces of such a violence.

The above describes, in very summary terms, the principal connecting thread of the book's five chapters, a thread which disappears in one place to resurface in another. A constant, however, is a focus on the constructions which enclose women with their desire. Whether it is behind the solid walls of the nun's cloister, at the unspoken limit of the hysteric's language, or within the frame set by a parent's desire, the passion that shapes these fictions can only discover itself in transgression of the law which encloses it. Moving beyond the limits of these constructions, Heloise and Mariana, the Princess de Clèves and Julie, Merteuil and Tourvel encounter many reasons to turn back: madness, danger, violence, betrayal, humiliation, and death. Nevertheless, as we read, we solicit the movement to the edge of the precipice, at this limit between our own desire and someone else's, reading always otherwise these fictions of woman's enclosure.

In the final two chapters of this study, we will begin to notice gestures of closure at the borders of the fictional work, where, in the liminal space of prefaces and forewords, postscripts and appendices, editorial commentary sets to work sealing cracks in the text. In the case of *Julie*, we come upon an editor hastening to cover over a "secret" that Julie—quite *naturally*—has disclosed. We glimpse here the possibility that the secrecy of the "secret" depends on the closing off of woman's desire. It is also our first hint that perhaps the most effective tool against this closure already lies at the reader's disposal: our indiscreet curiosity as we read another's mail. In *Les Liaisons Dangereuses*, it is again question of a secret that the editor would rather not reveal. The suspicions first roused by *Julie* are here confirmed: at stake in this definition of the limits of the book are the structures which keep women—and readers—in their place.

Telling secrets opens up these structures in another way as we approach the end of this book, since the hidden or buried term that surfaces cannot be identified only with the feminine pole in a static opposition. Rather, what may be most radically new in the new Heloise of the last two fictions is the link she provides in the differentiating force of desire which is denied by the boundaries set on the sexual distinction. Thus, if it is a woman's name that is buried by patriarchal singularity, retrieving that name will be at the same time the process of uncovering a connection to "Rousseau," which is then no longer quite so simply a man's name. In the final chapter, therefore, it cannot still be a question of feminine or masculine positions identified with the female or male characters. Instead, there are only liaisons between the points named Merteuil, Valmont, Tourvel, indeterminate spaces from which to write letters of disclosure.

As for the theoretical and interpretive framework within which I would insert my analyses, the connections once again remain implicit. Several constructs from psychoanalysis are perhaps most clearly to be seen, especially in the second chapter, where I suggest that *The Portuguese Letters* may be read as a case history of hysteria written in the first person of the hysteric rather than the analyst. The notes to each chapter draw out some of the other links with work related to my own. In general, however, what I have attempted here is a practice of reading that passes among the various levels of the text, that gives attention to detail, and that, instead of assigning meaning, looks for the terms which meaning excludes.[7] It is hoped that the reader unfamiliar with the theories of the text that such a technique implies will still see its interest for the reading of the particular works discussed here: narratives which stage the confrontation of a specific and active woman's desire with a social or symbolic order that represents no place for such a desire. Since each text elaborates a means with which to conceal the woman's passionate activity, that is, both to deny it and to assign it a (hidden) place in a structure, a reading that respects the already sanctioned categories of this structure—psychological, stylistic, or thematic, for example—can only continue to disguise the operation of the feminine in the text's language. To read without such respect for the boundaries dividing the estate of literary criticism is, perhaps, to begin to read differently—and at the risk of finding a woman's will in the undivided inheritance of our common lot.

1 / MARRIAGE CONTRACTS
The Letters of Heloise and Abelard

> The name of wife may seem more sacred or more binding, but
> sweeter for me will always be the word mistress, or, if you will
> permit me, that of concubine or even whore.
>
> Heloise to Abelard

> The pleasure they give is greater and more suitable for private
> than for public enjoyment, and their husbands take them into a
> bedroom and enjoy them rather than parade them before the
> world.
>
> Abelard to Heloise

The History

THE sketchy details of Abelard's confessional *Historia calamitatum*, or *Story of My Misfortunes*, suggest that Heloise and Abelard first met in 1117, probably in the cloister of Notre-Dame, within whose walls Heloise was then living with her uncle Fulbert and Abelard was the celebrated Master of the Cloister Schools of Paris. Under what circumstances they met is never recounted by either of them and we are left to wonder how they overcame the several obstacles of rule and convention which segregated men and women in both the scholastic and the ecclesiastical traditions that defined the cloister enclave. Each, however, was already known to the other by an unconventional reputation: Abelard, the brilliant dialectician and rhetorician, at age thirty-six or thirty-seven had arrived at the summit of a scholastic career by impudently taking on in dispute and soundly defeating his own masters in philosophy and theology—Guillaume de Champeaux and Anselm de Laon. His reputation was phenomenal and attracted an unprecedented number of students to his lectures from all over the continent. Of course, these students were, traditionally, all young men, since whatever education there was of girls could take place only in women's monasteries. It is for this reason that, at seventeen or eighteen, Heloise's own reputation as a scholar, by being the more unconventional, could rival

Abelard's. Thus, Abelard was not exaggerating too much when he recorded that her reputation preceded her "throughout the realm":

> There was in Paris at the time a young girl named Heloise, the niece of Fulbert, one of the canons, and so much loved by him that he had done everything in his power to advance her education in letters. In looks she did not rank lowest while in the extent of her learning she stood supreme. A gift for letters is so rare in women that it added greatly to her charm and had won her renown throughout the realm.[1]

Abelard recounts that after the defeat of Guillaume and Anselm, he felt invincible and exempt from the limits placed on other men. "I began to think myself the only philosopher in the world, with nothing to fear from anyone and so I yielded to the lusts of the flesh" (p. 65). Heloise was marked for his first conquest in this new field of sexual dialectics, which he approached armed with his "youth and exceptional good looks as well as [his] great reputation." It was a simple matter to flatter Fulbert's pride and get him to accept the master as private tutor for his niece and pensioner in his house. Abelard's plan to seduce his student was almost assured from the start, moreover, when this uncle turned over complete control of his niece to her tutor, even authorizing him to beat her if it became necessary.

> In handing her over to me to punish as well as to teach, what else was he doing but giving me complete freedom to realize my desires, and providing an opportunity, even if I did not make use of it, for me to bend her to my will by threats and blows if persuasion failed? [p. 67]

"Even if I did not make use of it"—that is, it did not prove necessary to beat Heloise in order to get what he wanted. Abelard suggests that, once installed in Heloise's house, he had no other obstacle to overcome and that his pupil yielded with no show of resistance: "Need I say more? We were united, first under one roof, then in heart."

The student-teacher relationship was quickly no more than a guise, a "pretext" for the other, secret, exchange. Part of this disguise was the violence which Fulbert was meant to interpret as a legitimate tool in the master's ascendancy over the disciple.

But that violence had another function as well within the erotic context, one which exceeded its meaning for Fulbert—discipline—and even its initial meaning for Abelard, which was very close to rape. In either of these senses, violence is the confirmation and visible sign of mastery. Erotic violence, however, breaks this univocal link:

> To avert suspicion I sometimes struck her, but these blows were prompted by love and tender feeling rather than anger and irritation, and were sweeter than any balm could be. In short, our desires left no stage of love-making untried, and if love could devise something new, we welcomed it. [Pp. 67–68]

In the later correspondence, Abelard pretended to ignore this ambiguity of pleasure in pain, eager as he was not only to reestablish his mastery over Heloise but also to erase her own association of violence with the erotic scene.

For several months, while Abelard and Heloise experimented with these pleasures, Fulbert remained convinced that they were pursuing more scholarly inquiries. When he finally could no longer ignore what all the rest of the city was openly discussing (Abelard writes that he circulated his love songs without disguising the name of his Lady, as was the courtly convention), Abelard was forced to leave Fulbert's house, although he continued to communicate with Heloise by letter and in surreptitious meetings. One of these meetings was interrupted when Fulbert came upon them, writes Abelard, "as the poet says happened to Mars and Venus" (p. 69). Soon after, Heloise wrote, in "a letter full of rejoicing," that she was pregnant. Abelard abducted his mistress from her uncle's home and, disguising her in a nun's habit, sent her to his sister in Brittany, where eventually a son was born and given the name Peter Astrolabe.

In Paris, meanwhile, Fulbert threatened Abelard with all manner of revenge but hesitated to carry out any of his plans since, in effect, Abelard was holding Heloise hostage. To break the deadlock and to appease Fulbert, Abelard went to him and accused himself of the deceit which love had made him commit, reminding the outraged uncle in the process "how since the beginning of the human race women had brought the noblest men to ruin" (p. 70). The situation, however, called for more than a rhetorical justification, and Abelard responded by offering to marry the dishonored girl. He added, however, the condition of secrecy, "so as not to damage [his] reputation." After Fulbert had accepted the proposal and its condition, Abelard left to carry the news to Heloise.

At this point, the history of Heloise and Abelard swerves into a dimension that marks a break with the events leading up to it. Whereas the seducer had encountered no resistance worth mentioning and the lover had been pulled into a vortex of erotic exploration which was not in his control, the suitor proposing marriage found himself confronted with a rhetorical barrage that attacked the rational ground of the proposal. Heloise's argument against this marriage is recounted in detail by Abelard (pp. 70–74), complete with supporting quotations from classical and biblical sources. Abelard would have us believe that Heloise studied more than *The Art of Love* with her preceptor, for the style here is unmistakably that of the academic dispute. She confronts Abelard with the rhetorical arms he had taught her to wield and in that moment he is forced to occupy the position into which he had once maneuvered Guillaume and Anselm: the master challenged in and by his own mastery. Clearly, this scene still rankled when—more than ten years later—Abelard set down its narration. In the middle of the tirade, and without acknowledging the transition, he drops the indices of attribution—"she said," "she argued"—and momentarily takes over the argument from his own current perspective as a celibate: "This is the practice today through love of God of those among us who truly deserve the name of monks" (p. 72). Writing as the monk he has become and no longer through indirect discourse, Abelard supplements Heloise's references to scripture and classical philosophy, reasserting his superior knowledge of the sources and taking over Heloise's ascendancy in the dispute. He also qualifies as "foolish obstinacy" his own imperviousness then to the force of Heloise's rhetoric, and even though he was somehow able to overcome her resistance, he records not a word of the counterargument he must have used at the time. One cannot help but wonder if Abelard did not finally find a proper use for the violence of the master that Fulbert had signed over to him.

Heloise's arguments against marriage have provoked almost

interminable commentary, beginning with the *Roman de la rose* at the end of the thirteenth century and with Jean de Meun's admiration for her frankness. Modern commentators have generally concentrated on reestablishing the argument's context and avoided judgments which risked anachronism.[2] Abelard, as "clerk and canon" (p. 73) in the church, had almost certainly taken no vow of chastity. These were minor titles, conferring more honorary than actual position. Celibacy was yet to be formalized as a requirement for the nonmonastic branch of the church hierarchy. It was, nevertheless, a requisite condition for those who, like Abelard, might be expected to occupy one of its higher offices.

Abelard relates that Heloise's argument was twofold: first, that her uncle would not be appeased even by their marriage, and, second, that Abelard would be disgraced. It is to this second point that Heloise devotes the greater part of her argument, for to win it she need only repeat what she had learned from Abelard: that man's highest vocation is philosophy; that the true philosopher is he who shuns all lower entanglements and pursuits which could distract him from this vocation; that marriage is one such entanglement which risks involving the scholar in the baser concerns of life. From a slightly different angle, Heloise also argues that a philosopher of Abelard's talents should belong to all mankind, not just to one woman. She warns him against yielding to incontinence, urging him "to guard against being sucked down headlong into this Charybdis, there to lose all sense of shame and be plunged forever into a whirlpool of impurity" (p. 73).[3] Nevertheless, it is clear that she rejects marriage primarily as an insult to philosophical purity rather than as a violation of chastity. The alternative she prefers, as suggested by the final remarks attributed to her, is a continuation of some form of their current relations where "[they] would find the joy of being together all the sweeter the rarer [their] meetings were" (p. 74). Her protest "that the name of mistress instead of wife would be dearer to her" is inconsistent, to say the least, with any celebration of chastity as either Christian virtue or a virtue of the philosopher and indicates to what extent Heloise's thinking strains at the limits of the categories she has inherited from Abelard.[4] Let us, however, set aside an analysis of this reasoning until we encounter it in its full force, in Heloise's first letter to Abelard.

When they returned to Paris, the lovers were married very discreetly and separated immediately. As Heloise had predicted, however, Fulbert was unhappy with the arrangement as it did not make public amends for his dishonor. To force Heloise and Abelard into the open, Fulbert and his family made known the fact of the marriage, but he only succeeded in forcing Heloise's repeated denials of this fact when confronted with the public's curiosity. According to Abelard, Fulbert then resorted to a more direct approach and tried to beat Heloise into acknowledging her secret publicly. As before, Abelard intervened by removing Heloise from her uncle's house, this time taking her to the convent at Argenteuil and giving her once again a religious habit to wear.

It was probably not at all unusual for women to take refuge in convents without professing vows, which is what it seems Abelard intended for Heloise to do. He stresses that the habit he gave her did not include a veil. Fulbert, however, apparently misunderstood this intention and suspected Abelard of trying to force Heloise to join an order, thereby annulling, in effect, their marriage vows. Having been robbed of his honor by Abelard, Fulbert sought retribution in a form which would leave the offender irreversibly disgraced.[5] And reasoning thus, he sent some of his men to bribe their way into Abelard's chambers in the middle of the night, tie him down, and castrate him.

Fulbert finally got the publicity he wanted. The punishment he had devised for Abelard's crime was quickly known throughout Paris. By his own account, Abelard became the object of considerable sympathy, but he nevertheless felt too ashamed to resume the position which had gained him such prestige in the world. He decided to withdraw from secular life into a monastic order, but not before he had made Heloise promise to do the same. "Heloise had already agreed to take the veil in obedience to my wishes and entered the convent" (p. 76). What is here somewhat ambiguously stated becomes clear in Heloise's first letter: not only did Abelard extract this agreement from her prior to his own vows, but he insisted that she precede him in the act. This detail will be given a much larger significance when Heloise comes to reflect on it more than ten years later.

The *Historia calamitatum*, after evoking Heloise's dramatic entrance into religious life (she is pictured as she mounted the altar intoning Cornelia's lament over the dead Pompey), goes on to narrate Abelard's controversial career as theologian, accused twice of heresy, and monastic reformer, persecuted by the monks he sought to reform. The affair with Heloise, culminating in Fulbert's vengeance, is but one chapter in this story of his misfortunes, the chapter which, by putting an end to his worldly associations, introduces the narrator into a new set of relationships where the sexual dimension plays no part. If there was any other commerce between Heloise and Abelard for the first ten years after they took vows, the *Historia calamitatum* makes no reference to it.

No doubt Heloise would have warranted no further mention at all if, in 1129, certain events had not presented the opportunity to reinscribe their former relationship within the limits prescribed by the monastic rule. In that year, the nuns at Argenteuil, where Heloise was by then prioress, were evicted by the political scheming of an abbot who wanted to add their rich monastery to those already under his purview. Along with her sisters, Heloise found herself on the street, a nun without a convent. At the same time, the monastery of the Paraclete, which Abelard had founded in 1124 and been forced to abandon in the wake of a confused scandal, still stood empty. The solution was obvious. Heloise became the first abbess of the Paraclete monastery and her installation was presided over by its founder and patron, Abelard, himself then abbott of St. Gildas Abbey in Brittany. Although technically still husband and wife, Heloise and Abelard were now related within the structure of the church, where their marriage could have only a metaphoric significance. This transition from a literal or worldly marriage to a figurative or spiritual one lies at the center of the debate in the correspondence.

The Letters

It would seem that Abelard remained several months at the Paraclete after Heloise's installation there. His departure was abrupt, caused once again by a scandal—local inhabitants were outraged by this monk setting up residence with his former mistress. A few years after Abelard returned to his own monastery in Brittany, he wrote the *Historia calamitatum*, in the form of a letter of consolation to a friend, and circulated several copies. Heloise's first personal letter to Abelard was supposedly prompted when she read one of these copies which "by chance someone brought her" (p. 109). By the terms of this letter, there seems to have been little or no contact between the nuns of the Paraclete and their founder, between the Abbess Heloise and the Abbott Abelard, since the latter had left several years before.

The correspondence between Heloise and Abelard is traditionally divided into two categories, the personal letters and the letters of direction. The first series consists of four letters—two from each of the correspondents—beginning with Heloise's response to reading the *Historia calamitatum*. The second series begins with another letter from Heloise in which she capitulates to Abelard's consistent substitution of the Christian symbolic context for the personal, erotic one and agrees to confine their communication to the discussion of theological issues or questions of monastic rule. Although these letters of direction constitute more than three-quarters of the total volume of the collection, we will consider only the four personal letters, as they provide the most lucid account of what interests us in Heloise's situation: the attempt to make a space for her erotic experience which does not reduce an unruly otherness—both hers and Abelard's—to a symbolic and ordered identity.[6] With her third letter—the first in the directional series—Heloise accepts the formal requirement which Abelard has made a condition of any further correspondence. But in doing so, she adopts an almost cynical tone, so that Abelard might know that her gift of obedience to his will is still one of form and not substance:

> I would not want to give you cause for finding me disobedient in anything, so I have set the bridle of your injunction on the words which issue from my unbounded grief; thus in writing at least I may moderate what it is difficult or rather impossible to forestall in speech. For nothing is less under our control than the heart— having no power to command it, we are forced to obey. And so when its impulses move us, none of us can stop their sudden promptings from easily breaking out, and even more easily overflowing into words which are the ever-ready indications of the

> heart's emotions. . . . I will therefore hold my hand from writing words which I cannot restrain my tongue from speaking; would that a grieving heart would be as ready to obey as a writer's hand! [P. 159]

As Etienne Gilson was perhaps the first to remark, this tepid agreement to moderate "the ever-ready indications of the heart's emotions" hardly constitutes the sort of conversion experience which might lead one to conclude that Abelard fabricated wholly or in part the correspondence as exemplum.[7] Such a conclusion can only be the result of a systematic misreading of Heloise's first two letters itself no different from the system which Abelard inaugurated in his own misreading of these same letters.[8]

Heloise's first letter to Abelard bears this superscription: "To her master, or rather her father, husband or rather brother; handmaid, or rather his daughter, wife or rather sister; to Abelard, Heloise" (p. 109). The repeated substitution of the monastic titles (father—brother/daughter—sister) for the secular ones (master—husband/handmaid—wife), as well as the shift from hierarchical terms (master—father/handmaid—daughter) to terms in which only the masculine/feminine distinction is pertinent (husband—brother/wife—sister), serves as eloquent introduction to the ambiguities of the letter which follows. The form of the superscription was not an empty convention for Heloise, as we learn in her second letter when she admonishes Abelard for having placed her own name before his on the superscription of his intervening letter. He had written: "To Heloise, his dearly beloved sister in Christ, Abelard her brother in Christ" (p. 119). "Surely," responds Heloise, "the right and proper order is for those who write to their superiors or equals to put their names before their own, but in letters to inferiors, precedence in order of address follows precedence in rank" (p. 127). Abelard's final letter in this series stubbornly persists on this point. It is addressed: "To the bride of Christ, Christ's servant" (p. 137). In that letter, Abelard explains that, while he agrees with the principle that Heloise has invoked, his first superscription was meant to reflect precisely the order of precedence which now pertains between them. Heloise, as the bride of Christ, shall come before Abelard, who is merely Christ's servant.

Returning, then, to the form of address of the first letter, in which Heloise alternates between so many qualifying modes of relationship, it is finally the simple order—"To Abelard, Heloise"—which overrides all the other distinctions. Heloise signals resolutely her position of inferior addressing her superior. It is the mode of address she will adopt for her second letter as well, although here she couches it in the language of Christian devotion: "To her only one after Christ, she who is his alone in Christ" (p. 127).[9]

In this quibbling over such a seemingly insignificant matter, Heloise and Abelard are drawing out the terms of their confrontation. For Heloise to acknowledge Abelard's deferral to her requires that she accept the symbolic order which confers that precedence and which gives its authority to the formula "To the bride of Christ, Christ's servant." Likewise, for Abelard to ignore Heloise's persistant reversal of his religious order is to invite a breach in that system where the erotic scene, with its violent interruption of mastery, can recur. Abelard, in other words, argues for woman's precedence as a necessary position within an order that stabilizes a singular mastery. Addressing Heloise as his superior is the formal preparation to retaining his rank in the body of the letters. On the other hand, in refusing the distinction, Heloise is attempting to revive the erotic confusion wherein mastery is posited only as a pretext to an evacuation of the controlling hierarchies.

In the first several paragraphs of the text of the letter, Heloise, writing as spokeswoman for her monastic community, represents to its founder a collective response to his *Historia calamitatum*. In the name of that community, she urges him to seek consolation in his obligations to these women and to find comfort in their readiness to assume part of the burden of his despair. The conventional device of the *Historia calamitatum*—a letter of consolation to a friend describing one's own great misfortunes—has had the contrary effect on these women, whose devotion to Abelard is second only to their devotion to God.

> You wrote your friend a long letter of consolation, prompted no doubt by his misfortunes, but really telling of your own. The detailed account you gave of these may have been intended for his

comfort, but it also greatly increased our own feelings of desolation; in your desire to heal his wounds you have dealt us fresh wounds of grief as well as re-opening the old. [P. 111]

In exactly the same manner, Heloise's long letter is prompted by Abelard's misfortunes but really tells of her own. The pretext of the collective response is dropped and Heloise proceeds to represent her own particular desolation. This shift is effected rhetorically through example, which also displaces the first person plural of the addressor with the singular.

Your superior wisdom knows better than our humble learning of the many serious treatises which the holy Fathers compiled for the instruction or exhortation or even the consolation of holy women, and of the care with which these were composed. And so in the precarious early days of our conversion long ago I was not a little surprised and troubled by your forgetfulness, when neither reverence for God nor our mutual love nor the example of the holy Fathers made you think of trying to comfort me, wavering and exhausted as I was by prolonged grief, either by word when I was with you or by letter when we had parted. [P. 112][10]

After making this transition, the letter never returns to its initial rhetorical position but sustains the particularized form of address: "To Abelard, Heloise." The rest of this letter, then, is calculated to oblige Abelard to respond in the same terms, to constrain him to address the woman for whom the obligations of a religious order are only a pretext.

Once Heloise has managed the transition from Abelard's obligation to the community of religious women—an obligation which is constituted within the ecclesiastical hierarchy—to his particular obligation to her, which has its only grounds in their experience as lovers, the model of contractual debt is displaced by another, far less limited, economy:

Yet you must know that you are bound to me by an obligation which is all the greater for the further close tie of the marriage sacrament uniting us, and are the deeper in my debt because of the love I have always borne you, as everyone knows, a love which is beyond all bounds. [Pp. 112–13]

This passage first evokes Abelard's relationship to Heloise in the bound and binding terms of marriage, which inaugurates contractual debt as the form of exchange between the partners. It is thus comparable to any other exchange—as, for example, that between the founder of a monastery and the monastic community—where debt is also the binding force. Here, however, the similarity ends, or rather is surpassed by Heloise's final formulation: a debt owed for a love which is "beyond all bounds." This formulation upsets the contractual model, for a contract is necessarily and by definition an institution of limits. A debt can be owed precisely because of the possibility of repayment. This possibility is a function of the prior limits set on the exchange, which is thus a bound exchange—that is, one which creates obligation to the extent that it limits it. The formulation of an *unbounded* obligation, on the other hand, by destroying the limit which alone gives meaning to the concept, undermines not only the terms of the comparison, but the very notion that Abelard is indebted to Heloise. A debt which knows no limit, which cannot be repaid, is no longer or not yet a debt.

We find here but the first formulation of the unremitting paradox of Heloise's discourse: in soliciting Abelard's debt to her unlimited love, she destroys that which binds him to her as far as it can be understood through comparison with limited models of exchange. This paradox has its rhetorical correlative: the device of the example, the elucidation of the general by means of comparison with the particular, is in fact what allows Heloise to insinuate a chasm of difference between the two terms she compares.

In the next paragraph, Heloise proceeds once again to overturn the terms of her exposition in order to follow the course of this transgressive economy:

> You alone have the power to make me sad, to bring me happiness or comfort; you alone have so great a debt to repay me, particularly now when I have carried out all your orders so implicitly that when I was powerless to oppose you in anything, I found strength at your command to destroy myself. I did more, strange to say—my love rose to such *heights of madness* that it robbed itself of what it most desired beyond hope of recovery, when immediately at your bidding I changed my clothing along with my mind, in order to prove you the sole possessor of my body and my will alike. [P. 113]

The "heights" of madness are scaled at the moment the meaning of a concept includes rather than excludes that which, within a limited economy of meaning, has an opposing value. For Heloise, one such moment occurs when desire immolates its object. Beyond all limits and all bounds, Heloise's entry into the convent cannot represent for her a conversion in the conventional sense for it is proof precisely of transgression of the convent's limits. Secular / monastic, chastity / licentiousness are clearly two of the oppositions which are set whirling in this boundlessness. Others no doubt are pulled into the imploding center of her reality, pulled in by the force of the erotic scene we have already encountered in its power to convert violence into something "sweeter than any balm could be."

As the paragraph proceeds, Heloise makes clear what she earlier left unstated: the limited economy of exchange, by defending against the madness she has just evoked, can account for only a degraded, covetous desire, desire as consumption.

> God knows I never sought anything in you except yourself; I wanted simply you, nothing of yours. I looked for no marriage-bond, no marriage portion, and it was not my own pleasures and wishes I sought to gratify, as you well know, but yours. [P. 113]

Beyond the limits of the contract, her pleasures and wishes are not exclusive and cannot be exchanged. We read Heloise's madness reiterating the model of the erotic transgression of the separation of two identities, two bodies. "You know, beloved, as the whole world knows, how much I have lost in you, how . . . that supreme act of flagrant treachery robbed me of myself in robbing me of you"; "My heart was not in me but with you, and now, even more, if it is not with you it is nowhere" (p. 117).

Heloise next elaborates a reversal and displacement of the opposition marriage and concubinage. This section opens with one of the sentences placed in epigraph: "The name of wife may seem more sacred or more binding, but sweeter for me will always be the word mistress, or, if you will permit me, that of concubine or even whore." Although Abelard had attributed a similar statement to Heloise in his representation of her argument against marriage in the *Historia*, she would seem to be dissatisfied with this representation. His long and detailed account omitted certain developments which, in retrospect at least, Heloise considers crucial.

> You thought fit to set out some of the reasons I gave in trying to dissuade you from binding us together in an ill-starred marriage. But you kept silent about most of my argument for preferring love to wedlock and freedom to chains. [P. 114]

We recall that Abelard represents Heloise's diatribe as nearly a point-for-point transposition of the classical and scriptural treatments of the theme. We have also noted that the logical consistency of that argument is undermined by the final position Abelard attributes to her: "Heloise then . . . argued that the name of mistress instead of wife would be dearer to her and more honourable for me—only love freely given should keep me for her, not the constrictions of a marriage tie" (p. 74).

Another reader of these texts underscores this inconsistency as proof that Abelard distorted Heloise's argument in order to ridicule her casuistry and demonstrate their shared hypocrisy. He writes:

> Heloise plays a delightful trick on her audience: she elaborates arguments concerning the disadvantages of marriage, but fails to carry through to its logical application to Abelard the argument in favor of continence. The result is a remarkable piece of medieval humor . . . Heloise, completely abandoning logic with a somewhat alarming feminine flair, is made to say that it would be "more pleasing" to her and "more virtuous" for him if she became his mistress rather than his wife.[11]

The logic that Heloise has "completely abandoned" is the contractual logic of limits which allows concepts to function, to have meaning through opposition. Instead, she passes from an equation of virtue and continence, with its contrary equation of disrepute and incontinence, to the formulation of a concubinage which is virtuous or honorable. This shift, however, has another consistency and is controlled by another "logic."[12]

When, many years later, Heloise again takes up her argument against marriage, she does so at the point which Abelard represents at the end of his account. She also makes clear that her version is a supplement by including a slightly amended quotation from Abelard's text:

> God is my witness that if Augustus, Emperor of the whole world,
> thought fit to honour me with marriage and conferred all the earth
> on me to possess for ever, *it would be dearer and more honourable to
> me* [*carius mihi et dignius videretur*] to be called not his Empress but
> your whore [*meretrix*]. [P. 114]

Abelard had written: "The name of mistress instead of wife
would be dearer to her and more honourable to me [*sibi carius existeret
mihique honestius*]." There is little point in speculating on which
of these two versions most correctly records Heloise's own
phrasing at the time of her famous diatribe. But it is clear that she
here reproaches him with a misrepresentation of her remarks
(Abelard does not answer her on this point in his letter of reply)
and cites a phrase of his, making a correction or a substitution.
By shifting the honorable epithet (*dignius* or *honestius*) from
Abelard to herself, from the master to the whore, Heloise, writing in her own name, exaggerates the inconsistency of her formulation and, at the same time, accuses the more timid syntax of
Abelard's indirect discourse. His account mitigates the confrontation of the two exclusive terms while Heloise first
maximizes the distance between wife and mistress with an
hyperbole (not just any man's wife but Augustus's, emperor of
the whole world) in order to give still greater force to the collapse
of the operative distinctions in the figure of the honorable
whore.

The rhetoric of the letters insists further on its own scandalous
logic by substituting for Abelard's term *amica*, which can be
translated as mistress or simply as friend, the word *meretrix*
which, in its vulgarity, is shocking regardless of the context. Yet
the context emphasizes the epithetical force of such a word for, as
Heloise has already made clear, its value for her is as a name, a
label: "Sweeter for me will always be the word [*vocabulum*]
mistress [*amica*], or, if you will permit me, that of concubine
[*concubina*], or [even] whore [*scortum*]."[13] The progression from
Abelard's term *amica* to the obscenity of *scortum* passes through a
challenge to the understanding of her correspondent—"if you
will permit me [*si non indigneris*; more literally, if you will not be
indignant or outraged]." Heloise is challenging him to follow her
in this undermining of the logical and linguistic categories that
oppose the epithet whore and the attributes of virtue or honesty.

The reversal or perversion of logic which Heloise sets in motion with the figure of the honorable whore is next displaced onto its complementary figure, that of the dishonorable wife:

> For a man's worth does not rest on his wealth or power; these depend on fortune, but worth on his merits. And a woman should realise that if she marries a rich man more readily than a poor one, and desires her husband more for his possessions than for himself, she is offering herself for sale. Certainly any woman who comes to marry through desires of this kind deserves wages, not gratitude, for clearly her mind is on the man's property, not herself, and she would be ready to prostitute herself to a richer man if she could.

From which it follows that such a wife is a whore for whom that epithet has its full odious connotation if not its denotative meaning. But it also follows that the mistress who can write to her lover "I wanted simply you and nothing of yours" is a whore in name only and one who, in embracing that name, gives proof of a love "beyond all bounds," beyond the bounded signs of a man's worth and a woman's honor.

We have already seen how Heloise displaces the limited economy of the marriage contract with an unlimited exchange that destroys the exclusive value of opposing terms. I have suggested that this unbinding of oppositions makes the link between a textual dynamic and a sexual one, between a rhetorical strategy and an erotic scene. That a letter could serve as a masked erotic scene is already a convention for both Heloise and Abelard, as we learn in the *Historia* when Abelard takes note of Heloise's literacy as a definite advantage in the woman he chooses to seduce: "When separated we could enjoy each other's presence by exchange of written messages in which we could speak more openly than in person and so need never lack the pleasures of conversation (p. 66). Heloise, for her part, has not forgotten these conversations with her lover, and her letter joins a request for consolation with this reminder: "When in the past you sought me out for sinful pleasures your letters came to me thick and fast" (p. 117). The erotic function of the letter is also marked by its place within scholastic pedagogy as the primary tool for the teaching of rhetoric. For Heloise and Abelard, that pedagogical scene is significant only insofar as it masks the other, erotic, one. "And so with our lesson as *pretext* we abandoned ourselves entirely to love. Her studies allowed us to with-draw in private, as love desired" (p. 67).

When we earlier came across this point in the narration of the seduction, it was apparent that Abelard's violence was meant to function, as he writes, "to avert suspicion," and that the hidden sexual context gave this violence its opposite meaning of "balm." What is not as apparent in Abelard's text, however, is the extent to which the erotic is experienced as indissociable from its pretext, from the false significance it offers to the world as represented by Fulbert. This becomes clear only in Heloise's letter, where Abelard's preeminence, his mastery, is never sub-jected to a reversal of the sort that her text performs on other hierarchical terms. "I believed that the more I humbled myself on your account, the more gratitude I should win from you, and also the less damage I should do to the brightness of your reputation" (p. 113). While she has been forced to modify this belief some-what when she considers Abelard's neglect ("Consider then your injustice, if when I deserve more you give me less, or rather, nothing at all" [p. 117]), she has yet to renounce it, and with it Abelard's mastery over her. To maintain the fiction of this mas-tery, as to continue the pedagogical pretext, is to keep alive the possibility of the erotic subtext in which neither is master. Only in this pretext of submission can she create a backstage for her desire within the public theater of its denial or its subjection.[14]

That Abelard's authority or mastery must remain intact as a fiction, preserved from the unbinding energies which this letter sets loose on other oppositions and hierarchies, does not prevent an analysis which points to this "error" or "delusion," but in a mediated fashion. This analysis begins when Heloise cites the advice of "the learned Aspasia" to a quarreling husband and wife, and then offers her commentary:

"Unless you come to believe that there is no better man nor wor-thier woman on earth you will always still be looking for what you judge the best thing of all—to be the husband of the best of wives and the wife of the best of husbands."

These are saintly words which are more than philosophic; in-deed, they deserve the name of wisdom, not philosophy. It is a holy error and a blessed delusion between man and wife, when perfect love can keep the ties of marriage unbroken not so much through

> bodily continence as chastity of spirit. But what error permitted
> other women, plain truth permitted me, and what they thought of
> their husbands, the world in general believed, or rather, knew to be
> true of yourself; so that my love for you was the more genuine for
> being further removed from error. [Pp. 114–15]

The "plain truth" was made evident by Abelard's fame, by the
public acclaim which, in the rest of this passage, is described as
unanimous. Unanimity characterized as well the judgment of
Abelard's desirability, his sexual worth: "Every wife, every
young girl desired you in absence and was on fire in your
presence; queens and great ladies envied me my joys and my
bed." The cast of Abelard's admirers is expanded to include even
the "unlettered," who, although they could not appreciate his
talents as a philosopher, were charmed by the words and
melodies of his love verses, such that once again these gifts
accrued to his sexual reputation: "And as most of these songs
told of our love, they soon made me widely known and roused
the envy of many women against me. For your manhood was
adorned by every grace of mind and body. . . . "

Heloise, in effect, gives the most forceful proof of her own
"holy error and blessed delusion" in this portrait of the "best of
husbands" where the superlative mode admits no dissent. Her
delusions about Abelard's preeminence have simply been displaced from their intimate context to a generalized and mediated
level where truth is a function of unanimity. This displacement
effectively reinstates the public domain as the domain of pretense and pretext to the erotic "truth."

Public opinion, however, reverts to an exclusive determination of truth as soon as the erotic disruption is blocked. In the
case of Heloise and Abelard, this interruption brutally coincides
with Abelard's castration. It is in the aftermath of this event that
public opinion again becomes the locus of an invulnerable, generalized truth which, by reinstating the limits of exchange,
stabilizes the pretense of Abelard's mastery and Heloise's submission into an oppressive reality.

> Tell me one thing, if you can. Why, after our entry into religion,
> which was your decision alone, have I been so neglected and
> forgotten by you that I have neither a word from you when you are
> here to give me strength nor the consolation of a letter in absence?

Tell me, I say, if you can—or I will tell you what I think and indeed
the world suspects. It was desire, not affection, which bound you to
me, the flames of lust rather than love. So when the end came to
what you desired, any show of feeling you used to make went with
it. This is not merely my own opinion, beloved, it is everyone's.
There is nothing personal or private about it; it is the general view
which is widely held. [P. 116]

What is so loathsome to Heloise about this opinion is that it
places a contractual definition on that which has its only force, its
only being, in an effacement of such definitions. It is for the same
reason that Heloise describes herself as having been overwhelmed with shame when Abelard insisted that she precede
him into holy orders:

When you hurried towards God I followed you, indeed I went first
to take the veil—perhaps you were thinking how Lot's wife turned
back when you made me put on the religious habit and take my
vows before you gave yourself to God. Your lack of trust in me over
this one thing, I confess, overwhelmed me with grief and shame. I
would have had no hesitation, God knows, in following you or
going ahead at your bidding to the flames of Hell. [P. 117]

Abelard's action takes its meaning from the economy of contractual limits to which it assigned their exchange. Seeing her
precede him into the convent stabilizes the order of mastery and
submission and negates the destabilizing experience of the erotic. Heloise's act is thereby doubly marked as a submission to an
order that denies her desire. To this degraded and degrading
version of their union—in which all her fears concerning marriage are realized—Heloise can only respond with another image
of transgressed limits: "following you or going ahead at your
bidding to the flames of Hell."[15]

Heloise employs the contractual model of debt and obligation
in order to solicit the erotic infraction of these terms. However,
insofar as this model is stabilized and grounded in the limit
imposed by Abelard's castration, her solicitation disregards this
fact of castration. Her error or delusion allows her to address
Abelard at a point which lies outside any reference to his mutilation and to appeal to him for that which, in the limited sense, he
is no longer able to give. This accounts, in part, for the unrea-
sonableness of this letter, which will become even more evident
when she must reply to the too-reasonable tone and terms of

Abelard's response. In her next reply, Heloise poses her desire as an unaccounted-for excess within the exchange Abelard proposes. Here, however, she is operating as if such a limited exchange can still function as pretext to the erotic transgression. She is thus able to assign acceptable terms to her desire within that language of exchange:

> I beg you then to listen to what I ask—you will see that it is a small favour which you can easily grant. While I am denied your presence, give me at least through your words—of which you have enough to spare—some sweet semblance of yourself. It is no use my hoping for generosity in deeds if you are grudging in words. [P. 116]
>
> I beg you to restore your presence to me in the way you can—by writing me some word of comfort. [P. 117]

Abelard's reply, the second letter in the series, counters Heloise's rhetorical strategy with a strategy of its own. He responds selectively to the ambiguities of her request for consolation, making clear that he can offer only the sort of aid authorized by their spiritual relation: "If . . . you feel that you have need of my instruction and writings *in matters pertaining to God*, write to me what you want, so that I may answer *as God permits me*" (p. 119). As for Heloise's complaints about his neglect, Abelard excuses himself with a polite explanation:

> If since our conversion from the world to God I have not yet written you any word of comfort or advice, it must not be attributed to indifference on my part but to your own good sense, in which I have always had such confidence that I did not think anything was needed. [P. 119]

Abelard risks this reasoning even though it is itself the object of a complaint for Heloise, who had written: "If only your love had less confidence in me, my dear, so that you would be more concerned on my behalf! But as it is, the more I have made you feel secure in me, the more I have to bear with your neglect" (p. 117). Surely Abelard would have noticed that Heloise was at that same moment contradicting her accusation immediately preceding of a "lack of trust," an accusation which arises when she remembers the order of their vows. The strategy of Abelard's response, however, is to avoid being drawn into the inconsistencies or flawed logic of Heloise's text, those moments of flagrant transgression of conceptual limits. Instead, he pursues his own error or delusion, writing *as if* his former pupil had no knowledge of the erotic contradiction of appearances. His reply acknowledges only this appearance and not its potential contravention.

Thus, in the rest of the letter, he writes as spiritual adviser to the monastery, reminding the Abbess Heloise of the scriptural precedents which demonstrate the special power of women's prayers to win mercy from the Lord. He presents a cluster of biblical examples, illustrating the number of times women interceded successfully for the men they loved. It is such an intercession on his own behalf that Abelard hopes Heloise and her sisters will make the object of their prayers. He then details the dangers he confronts among the hostile monks in Brittany—several attempts have already been made on his life, and his enemies give no sign of renouncing their efforts. The letter ends with instructions concerning his request to be buried at the Paraclete and to be remembered after his death in the offices of the order. The evocation of his death concludes with a final example of the woman's special role in the performance of these services: he reminds Heloise that it was women who laid Christ in the grave, kept watch at his tomb, and gave first witness to the resurrection.

Abelard's selective reading of her first letter forces Heloise to adopt less ambiguous terms for her second. She makes explicit the contradictions which Abelard overlooks and formalizes them in the figure of her own hypocrisy. She also abandons an implicit evocation of the erotic scene in favor of graphic images of their sexual encounters. She again employs the tactic of grafting a more intimate dialogue onto the exchange between an abbess and her superior, but this time makes it far more difficult for Abelard to respond without acknowledging the intimate reference.

We have already discussed the opening of this letter: Heloise's reproval of Abelard's superscription. From this reproach concerning the order of precedence, her letter leads into a somewhat different but related consideration of order. Citing Abelard's instructions for his burial at the Paraclete, Heloise protests that such foresight tortures the community with the idea that they might survive their master.

> The proper course would be for you to perform our funeral rites, for you to commend our souls to God, and to send ahead of you those whom you assembled for God's service—so that you need no longer be troubled by worries for us, and follow after us the more gladly because freed from concern for our salvation. [P. 128]

It is hard not to read in this evocation a repetition of the passage from a worldly to a contemplative life, the passage which is marked for Heloise by a certain order.

Through this reference, the letter already anticipates the moment at which it will take up the matter of her conversion: "At every stage of my life up to now, God knows, I have feared to offend you rather than God, and tried to please you more than him. It was your command, not love of God which made me take the veil" (p. 134). This failure to convert her love for Abelard into a love of God—despite Abelard's implicit comparison of his death and burial with Christ's—is at the root of that failure of prayer that Heloise anticipates when she counters Abelard's evocation of his death with her own vision of the scene:

> What time will there be then which will be fitting for prayer, when extreme distress will allow us no peace, when the soul will lose its power of reason and the tongue its use of speech? Or when the frantic mind, far from being resigned, may even (if I may say so) rage against God himself, and provoke him with complaints instead of placating him with prayers? [P. 128]

It is in almost the same terms that Heloise later describes her failed penitence:

> I can find no penitence whereby to appease God, whom I always accuse of the greatest cruelty in regard to this outrage. By rebelling against his ordinance, I offend him more by my indignation than I placate him by making amends through penitence [P. 132]

Heloise's failed conversion is the unbroken thread which organizes this letter. Unlike material conversion, which is the process of transforming one substance into another, spiritual conversion can only be understood as the function of a reevaluation, that is, it is not the terms themselves which are changed but the values or meanings assigned to them: negative value replaces positive value or positive negative. It is this process of reevaluation which has not overtaken Heloise's discourse about her past and hence her present. This also contributes to the anomaly which we turned up in the first letter: her disregard, on a certain level, of Abelard's castration. In effect, nothing has been changed or converted for Heloise. The only level at which the castration is recognized is one in which it has the value of loss ("how much I have lost in you, how at one wretched stroke of fortune that supreme act of flagrant treachery robbed me of my very self in robbing me of you"). Heloise has not performed the act of interpretation which converts that loss into a gain, the wound into a healing grace, to use the terms of Abelard's second letter. Her desire remains intact, as does the object of that desire—regardless of the loss suffered in reality. The conversion of that loss is possible only through reference to a system outside the one created by her desire. However, as we have already seen, the possibility of such a reference is canceled by the transgressive relation of desire to its "outside," which is always available to serve as pretext. There is no point safely beyond such ever-expanding limits on which to ground a negation, no concept or intention which can effectively oppose or exclude desire. This is more than a logical dilemma for Heloise. She experiences it as a form of madness.

In the absence of a conversion which could stabilize and thus exclude desire, Heloise's text remains caught in a highly unstable movement of contradiction. The only constant she can propose is one which formalizes this instability without reducing it: hypocrisy. However, before the letter arrives at this formulation, it passes through a succession of reversals.

In the initial formulation, Heloise is "of all wretched women . . . the most wretched, and amongst the unhappy . . . the unhappiest" (p. 129). These superlatives are correlated with the greatest happiness Heloise had known with Abelard. This hyperbolic rhetoric, moreover, only reflects the fate which Fortune had devised—a classical lesson in *hubris*: "that the happiness of supreme ecstasy would end in the supreme bitterness of sorrow" (p. 130). When Heloise next considers why she might deserve such a severe reprimand, she first sees only the injustice of the punishment, coming as it did after the lovers had made amends by submitting to the rite of marriage and after they had separated to lead a life "which was holy as well as chaste." What is more, she writes to Abelard, "you alone were punished, although we are both to blame, and you paid all, though you had deserved less, for you had made more than necessary reparation by humbling yourself on my account and had raised me and all my kind to your own level."

From this protest of injustice, Heloise passes to the evidence of the guilt of woman, whose general lot is "to bring total ruin on great men." She considers several scriptural warnings against the Circe-like dangers of her sex, and then recites the Old Testament list of great men brought low by women: Adam, Samson, Solomon. Not without some logical contortions, she concludes that Satan arranged her marriage to Abelard because he knew how easily wives could destroy their husbands: he "attacked you by means of marriage when he could not destroy you through fornication" (p. 131). Heloise's guilt, then, originates in the moment she became Abelard's wife, the moment she allowed him to humble himself on her account. Thus, having begun with the fact of marriage as proof of heaven's injustice, Heloise passes with no apparent break to the fact of marriage as source of guilt.

This is not the final reversal but only establishes a momentary resting place within the spiral of contradictions. Heloise cannot totally assume blame for Abelard's misfortune since "no consent of [hers] makes [her] guilty of this crime." The term "consent" has a double sense here as both intention informing an act (to bring ruin on Abelard) and consent to marriage. While Heloise may find herself innocent on both counts—did she not try to dissuade Abelard from marrying by predicting his ruin?—she nevertheless puts forth yet another image of her guilt: "I yielded long before to the pleasures of carnal desires" (p. 132).

Having finally located desire as the guilty term, Heloise makes no move to negate it through yet another reversal: "The sequel is a fitting punishment for my former sins, and an evil beginning must be expected to come to a bad end" (p. 132).[16] Yet her letter does fail to convert this confession into a renunciation when it refuses the image of the penitent which this exposition elicits. Whatever reparation she has made is in view of appeasing, not

God, but Abelard for the humiliation he has suffered. Her penitence, therefore, for the sin of desire cannot be distinguished from that sin which Heloise at one point describes in these terms: "I believed that the more I humbled myself on your account, the more gratitude I should win from you."

That this desire is inescapable, that it cannot be negated or excluded even as one denounces it, maintains Heloise at a constant distance from the renunciation which would accompany a conversion. Indeed, the structural opposition which signifies this renunciation—mortification of the flesh in the place of pleasures of the flesh—is ineffectual since mortification has already come to signify pleasure. "How can it be called repentance for sins, however great the mortification of the flesh, if the mind still retains the will to sin and is on fire with its old desires?" (p. 132). There is no sanctuary, no structure which can lock out the invasion of erotic forms, erotic significance. Neither the symbolic activity of the Mass nor the meaningless inactivity of sleep can function to contain or convert the repetition of the erotic scene.

> In my case the pleasures of lovers which we shared have been too sweet—they can never displease me, and can scarcely be banished from my thoughts. Wherever I turn they are always there before my eyes, bringing with them awakened longings and fantasies which will not even let me sleep. Even during the celebration of the Mass, when our prayers should be purer, lewd visions of those pleasures take such a hold upon my unhappy soul that my thoughts are on their wantonness instead of on prayers. I should be groaning over the sins I have committed, but I can only sigh for what I have lost. Everything we did and also the times and places are stamped on my heart along with your image, so that I live through it all again with you. Even in sleep I know no respite. Sometimes my thoughts are betrayed in a movement of my body, or they break out in an unguarded word. [P. 131]

The figure of the hypocrite which Heloise puts in place ("Men call me chaste; they do not know the hypocrite I am") follows on this portrait of disrupted appearances. With it, the letter responds directly to Abelard's professed confidence in her "good sense." Her rejection of this commonplace but no less unwarranted praise is categorical. "For a long time my pretence deceived you, as it did many, so that you mistook my hypocrisy for piety" (p. 134). There follows a series of exhortations which urge Abelard to look beyond her pretence to what is dissimulated: "Do not feel so sure of me . . . do not suppose me healthy . . . do not believe I want for nothing . . . do not think me strong." Her letter accuses Abelard's error, which stabilizes appearance so as not to see the erotic instability. Her fantasies are thrust before him on the page. Heloise, it would seem, by attacking the too-well-defined reflection of herself which she reads in his letter, is attempting to resurrect another image which is not contained in Abelard's mirror. Continually disrupting the placid, sleeping exterior, her desire is that which such a mirror cannot be positioned to capture.

The protest of her hypocrisy—its confession not to God, but to Abelard—parallels dangerously an attempt at seduction. Heloise is seeking to draw Abelard out from behind the mirror with which he steadies her image so that he might once again fall within her own erotic frame: "Give me at least through your words . . . some sweet semblance of yourself." With these words, and with this semblance, will it not be possible to create yet another pretext, to derive yet another balm from their violence? The depravity which Heloise depicts for her correspondent—the "lewd visions" and the "wantonness"—contrives to call down the anger of the outraged master who discovers laxity in his pupil. She even suggests the form his response should take with a quotation from Ecclesiastes: "The sayings of the wise are sharp as goads, like nails driven home." Her commentary is equally suggestive: "That is to say, nails which cannot touch wounds gently, but only pierce through them" (p. 135). If words are all that Abelard has left to give her, let them pierce like nails.[17]

Abelard, the formidable rhetorician, must have read this letter as an implicit challenge to his powers of argument. His earlier tactic—the simple evasion of intimate exchange—is impracticable since Heloise has not followed suit but has raised her own stake in an eroticized exchange. His response this time will be one which appropriates the erotic while at the same time disarming its subversive potential.

As we have remarked, Abelard's earlier letter rigorously avoids being drawn into Heloise's transgressive logic. This letter, however, opens by stating its contrary intention: to analyze the structure of her text and to reply systematically to each element of this structure. "The whole of your last letter is given up to a recital of your misery over the wrongs you suffer, and these, I note, are on four counts: . . . I have decided to answer you on each point in turn" (p. 137). This dispassionate procedure signals Abelard's deference to a higher authority "so that," as he writes to Heloise, "you will more willingly grant my own requests when you understand that they have a basis in reason." By setting out to follow the logic of Heloise's letter, his reply cannot fail to dismiss its illogic, but this dismissal is concealed by the proposed analysis of "each point in turn." The selectiveness of Abelard's response disappears behind these two interdependent principles: the authority of reason and the comprehensiveness of analytic logic.

The "four counts" which Abelard discerns are, following the order of Heloise's letter: the question of the superscription; the evocation of his death; the manner of their entry into religious life; Abelard's unwarranted praise of her. As we shall see, Abelard follows this order for his own reply until he reaches the third point, which he chooses to take up last after skipping ahead to point four. This procedural lapse is not explained nor even acknowledged. That his analysis allows such a lapse, however, underscores one of its important assumptions: that Heloise's letter addresses four separate complaints which need not be considered in their relation to each other. By leaving out of account the transitions from one point to the next, Abelard's reply contrives to ignore what we have seen to be the unifying principle of Heloise's text: the failed negation or conversion of desire.

We have already summarized Abelard's justification for his choice of superscription. His argument for giving Heloise precedence finds its proof in the exegesis of passages from the *Song of Songs* which evoke the figure of the bride, in particular this verse: "I am black but lovely, daughters of Jerusalem; therefore the king has loved me and brought me into his chamber."[18] Abelard's exegetical skills are brought fully into play as he develops a highly complex analogy between the "black but lovely" bride of Scripture and Heloise's special status as a monastic woman.[19] Her black exterior, that is, the coarseness of the nun's black habit, is the sign of its hidden contrary: a beautiful white interior, just as the Ethiopian woman's dark skin contrasts with her white bones. Thus "as regards exterior appearance," she is "less lovely" than the other daughters of Jerusalem; yet what her coarse skin or veil hides is more beautiful. This analogy reveals in turn two other contrasting pairs: black as the sign of adversity or affliction, white as the contrary symbol of prosperity; also "the bones within . . . can properly stand for the soul" while "the flesh without" signifies nothing beyond its visible materiality.

On all its several levels, the analogy turns on the reversal of manifest appearance and hidden truth, resulting in formulations of the sort "black but lovely." The contradiction, however, is resolved through a hierarchization of the terms: not only the *hidden* but the *higher* truth of the soul and its virtues, of that which is visible only to God and apparent only once the body is shed like a veil. With this structure of reversal in place, Abelard does not hesitate to explicate how the sexual term functions within the comparison. Like the bride, the contemplative woman finds pleasure only in retreat from the public view which qualifies her blackness as a "disfigurement." The monastic seclusion, "where prayer can be offered more purely and quietly," is like that closed chamber where the king takes pleasure with the bride whose beauty is only revealed in this retreat. Abelard, by the same token, seems to take pleasure in drawing out this condition of the analogy. Heloise, like the Ethiopian bride, has been "led by the King of Heaven himself into his chamber and [rests] in his embrace, and with the door always shut [is] wholly given up to him, [is] more intimately bound to him" (p. 142).

As we remarked at the beginning of our analysis of the correspondence, the argument over the superscription is central to the confrontation played out in the course of these four letters. Clearly, Abelard is using Heloise's protest over his form of address as a pretext to respond in a displaced manner to her complaints. The care with which he elaborates the analogy of the black bride, superimposing her portrait on Heloise's until the two images coincide in every detail, is explained as soon as one gauges the extent to which Abelard is anticipating the other points of his response.[20]

Specifically, the analogy of the black bride replies already to what Heloise has written of her inescapable desire and consequent hypocrisy. In effect, Abelard reinscribes that desire and its force of contradiction in a mode which converts term for term the portrait Heloise sketches of herself. His counter-portrait follows the outlines of the double image but that superimposition eradicates the charge of hypocrisy even as it preserves its formal structure. The opposition manifest/hidden, which in Heloise's confession constitutes a guilty—even depraved— structure, is appropriated in the "black but lovely" topos as the index of sanctification, the discrepancy which is the sign of God's elect. In other words, Abelard's rehabilitation through analogy differs only in appearance and not in kind. It is not the structure of hypocrisy which is converted but the value placed on it.

If we look closely, however, at Abelard's appropriation of Heloise's contradiction, we find that a shift has occurred which marks it as a theft. For Heloise, as we recall, her own desire cannot be reconciled with an appearance and an opinion that are public currency and by virtue of which she usurps the praise reserved for chaste women. Yet, in Abelard's superimposed image of the black bride, it is the husband's desire, not the bride's, which reveals this discontinuity between a public and private discourse, a manifest and hidden reality. The shift from chaste but wanton to "black but lovely" is the shift from the description of a willed state (either wantonness or chastity), and therefore the attribution of a certain desire, to the description of objective qualities which are differentiated along the axis of another's desire (either absent or present). The contradiction "black but lovely" is only apparent since the two attributes do not coexist in the same space but are distributed between the scenes of public display and private enjoyment. The differentiating term is the husband's desire, which is also therefore not in conflict with itself.

> Moreover it often happens that the flesh of black women is all the softer to touch though it is less attractive to look at, and for this reason the pleasure they give is greater and more suitable for private than for public enjoyment, and their husbands take them into the bedroom to enjoy them rather than parade them before the world. [P. 140]

This passage articulates the noncontradiction of the bride's lovely blackness without invoking the concept of her beautiful but hidden soul. Instead, the duality has surfaced, so to speak, for the distinction public/private now corresponds to two equally true properties of her sensible reality: the color and the texture of her skin. This redistribution rotates the axis of a vertical description—the manifest appearance of the black skin which conceals the interiority of the white bones or soul— towards the horizontal axis of a contiguous surface. What, in the vertical analogy, is first supposed of an unobservable interiority is here made manifest through the skin, where it can be directly apprehended—and enjoyed. At the same time, necessarily, as this interiority disappears on the surface of the bride's body, it is redefined in the context of the husband's pleasure. Or rather, that pleasure is the agency of perception—seeing or touching—that organizes space into public and private, or exterior and interior, and that articulates this distinction on the body of his mate. Her body, in other words, is the objective representation of this other's desire which can, without contradiction, pass between private pleasures and public parade.

The pursuit of the analogy has led Abelard far afield of his starting point: the order of precedence which now obtains between himself and Heloise. The argument quickly loses sight of this question and does not return to it before moving on to the next point in its rebuttal. Clearly, the force of Abelard's rhetoric has another target. The analogy can function to displace Heloise's hypocrisy because it appears to sanction—even sanctify—the contradiction of appearances. Moreover, this sanction is tied not only to the reduction of the interiority of her desire but also to its reappropriation within a noncontradictory masculine space. Through this reappropriation, however, another scene drifts unacknowledged into view—the scene of a much earlier confrontation between the two lovers.

Among the brides whose "husbands take them into a bedroom to enjoy them rather than parade them before the world" we recognize Heloise in her role as Abelard's clandestine wife. Thus, what is puzzling in the account of the secret marriage from the *Historia*—why Abelard, unlike Heloise, did not recognize the futility of this stratagem to appease Fulbert—may perhaps find some explanation in the terms of our reading of the analogy. While it cannot represent an acceptable reparation in Fulbert's terms, the clandestine marriage sets up a structure within which Abelard's desire reappropriates control of its own interiority.[21] The condition of secrecy, imposed by Abelard, provides for a distinct distribution of public and private space. This condition, at the same time as it makes a place for the affirmation of desire, sets a definite limit on this affirmation and contains it within an opposition. This interpretation does not overlook the fact that commentators have repeatedly linked Abelard's insistence on secrecy with his ambition. In effect, by enclosing his erotic impulsion (and its object) within the walls of secrecy, he is seeking to contain that which subverts his master's discourse in the public domain.[22] Like that of the husband-king of the analogy, Abelard's desire remains interior to itself, that is, within the limits it has created and where it can be deployed without contradiction. When the secret arrangement threatened to collapse, as a result of Fulbert's manipulations, Abelard responded by placing Heloise in the cloister, thus reinforcing the necessary boundary between the public or secular domain and the hidden interior, where desire is revealed in the presence of its object. At this further remove from public view, he can once again give himself over without risk to those "private delights" which, if allowed into the open, would dismantle control of the structure. The cloister, by virtue of its physical and dogmatic seclusion from the world, can thus become, like the king's bedroom in the analogy, the favored scene of enjoyment. That it did in fact for Abelard is confirmed later in this letter:

> After our marriage, when you were living in the cloister with the nuns at Argenteuil and I came one day to visit you privately, you know what my uncontrollable desire did with you there, actually in a corner of the refectory, since we had nowhere else to go. I repeat, you know how shamelessly we behaved on that occasion in so hallowed a place, dedicated to the most holy Virgin. [P. 146]

As we have already seen, the black bride analogy reduces contradiction by substituting for the open confrontation of two different but mutually implicating locales of desire a singular space that is circumscribed and contained by an undifferentiated masculine will articulated on the unidimensional surface of a woman's body. In effect, then, Abelard's first response to the renewed threat of Heloise's desire is a displaced repetition of her earlier cloistering. What we thus see taking shape here is the initial movement of another logical exposition, one which underlies the announced structure of this letter. Before it can lead Heloise to an acceptance of castration and, thereby, to a starting point for the conversion of her own desire, the letter first reappropriates that desire to a noncontradictory masculine space. Abelard, in other words, proclaims the end of his desire only after reestablishing its ascendancy and its control. It is in this fashion that the castration is recuperated as the realization of a fantasmatic mastery of desire. In the process, castration becomes the index of a mastery which is unassailable and intact.

After this opening movement, which detours Heloise back into the cloister, the letter proceeds to block all the exits. The appeal to logic is the screen through which Heloise's letter is passed and which disarticulates the counter-logic of seduction. What is retained by this screen is not the self-undermining discourse of desire but one rather in which word coincides with intention, act with will, outer sign with inner meaning.[23] It is, of course, precisely this coincidence of meaning which eludes Heloise and which she exposes as her hypocrisy. In our analysis of this section of her letter, we understood Heloise to be subverting the flattened / flattered image of herself in an attempt to reactivate the disjunctive, delimiting operation of desire. Abelard counters this attempt in several stages: first, with the analogy of the black bride, as we have already seen; next, with an analysis of false modesty.

Abelard defines Heloise's fourth complaint (which he takes up out of order) as follows: "Lastly, you set your self-accusations against my praise of you, and implored me with some urgency not to praise you again" (p. 137). The form which these self-accusations have taken—briefly, the persistence of the erotic attachment to Abelard—is never directly cited in this review. Rather, Abelard sidesteps the dangerous evocation of the erotic scene and replaces it with a far less alarming threat:

> I approve of your rejection of praise, for in this very thing you show yourself more praiseworthy. . . . May your written words be re-

flected in your heart! If they are, yours is true humility and will not vanish with anything I say. But be careful, I beg you, not to seek praise when you appear to shun it, and not to reject with your lips what you desire in your heart. [Pp. 143–44]

In this passage, the slippage from the contradiction which Heloise has put in place to the one which Abelard warns her against is all the more difficult to remark because Abelard's response appears to repeat her formulation almost term for term. Heloise had used the same distinction between an outward display of rejection and a contrary inward embrace when she accused her own failed repentance:

It is easy enough for anyone to confess his sins, to accuse himself, or even to mortify his body in outward show of penance, but it is very difficult to tear the heart away from hankering after its dearest pleasures. [P. 132]

The difference is that those "dearest pleasures" cannot be limited to the sort of praise which Abelard invokes. Moreover, when he cautions her "not to reject with [her] lips what [she] desire[s] in [her] heart," he suppresses the fact that it is precisely in these terms that Heloise rejects his praise as unwarranted. Heloise's effort to step outside the frame of the mirror which reduces the dimension of her desire to a static appearance is recuperated through this suppression. In effect, Abelard contrives to dismiss Heloise's self-accusation of hypocrisy as a form of false modesty, an attempt to draw his praise.

But there is more at stake here than saving Heloise from a guilty humility. At an implicit level, Abelard recognizes the seductive potential of Heloise's attempt to engage him outside the boundaries of his discourse and the consequent danger to the structured stability of this frame of reference. Through his choice of an analogy, he concedes that Heloise seeks more from him than praise:

Such artfulness Virgil describes in wanton Galatea who sought what she wanted in flight, and by feigning rejection led on her lover more surely towards her: "She flees to the willows and wishes first to be seen." Before she hides she wants to be seen fleeing, so that the very flight whereby she appears to reject the youth's company ensures that she obtains it. [P. 144]

Like the black bride analogy, this one turns on a distinction between an apparent and a concealed level of signification. Within this repetition, however, the examples of the black bride and Galatea are clearly meant to oppose each other. Galatea's flight—her movement from one place to another, which initiates the same movement in her lover—has no complement in the other schema, where, as we read, the only implied motion is the husband-king's passage between public and private space, between the delights of the world and those of the bedroom. But Galatea, "who sought what she wanted in flight and . . . led on her lover more surely towards her," disturbs the stable binarism of this structure in several ways.

First, wishing her flight first to be seen, she confuses the distinction between the visible and the hidden. Her becoming-hidden is observed, so that, momentarily, she exists in some dubious margin where what is hidden is still seen and what is seen is already hidden. Second, this confusion at the margin cannot be contained there since, in order to occur at all, it must already exist as a possibility even before it assumes form in the observed flight from the visible. In other words, for the flight to suspend the opposition revealed/concealed, the meaning of each term has already to be contaminated with the meaning of the other. Third, just as this contamination cannot be contained within some spatial or temporal margin, Galatea's flight cannot be understood through reference to a meaningful context. Rather, the impulsion of desire both constitutes the opposition of its (necessary) context and overturns the opposition in the same movement. That movement must also, then, disarticulate the husband-king's fiction of the proper context for erotic pleasure. Finally, therefore, but perhaps most pertinently, Galatea's flight suspends the opposition between subject and object of desire. The syntax is ultimately undecidable because the flight and the pursuit are both feigned. In that appearance of a struggle between hunter and prey, each mocks the other's role, each agrees to play the other's fool. Like the other oppositions in this analogy, the hunter/hunted polarity—with its connotations of violence and force—is put into position only in order to be suspended, effaced in an erotic undecidability.[24]

In the figure of "wanton Galatea," we cannot fail to recognize the Heloise already encountered in our reading of her two letters. It is tempting to speculate that Abelard produced the analogy out of the same recognition, and that the variation on Virgil's theme represents his own brief flight into some fantasied willows.[25] But as wish or fantasy, it also represents, for the reasons we have just elaborated, a threat to whatever would—like the husband-king—keep a steady hand on the oppositions that in turn sustain a rule of public and domestic space. Coming out of his dream, the dreamer denies that he has wished for any such thing. "I mention this because it is a common occurrence, not because I suspect such things of you; I have no doubts about your humility" (p. 144). The danger, however, is not completely disarmed by the mechanism of denegation since that threat originates in a point of juncture with the subjectivity of another, in an intersection which is neither wholly internal nor completely external to the threatened subject. An adequate defense must include a suppression of this exterior locus: "But I want you to refrain from speaking like this so that you do not appear to those who do not know you so well to be seeking fame by shunning it" (p. 144). As Abelard here invokes the master's prerogative, he concedes that such authority is precariously built on an exclusion. The proscription silences precisely that which suspends univocal authority in an erotic margin. By directing Heloise "to refrain from speaking like this," Abelard enjoins her to dissimulate her desire more efficiently, so that it leaves no traces on the surface of things, no mark which belies the order of flight and pursuit, no sign which accuses the discrepancy within representation.

With the solicitation "May your written words be reflected in your heart," Abelard insinuates an identity into the gap that sustains Heloise's contradiction and her desire. This technique of recuperating contradiction has as its ultimate aim to restore a stable specularity within which mastery may reflect (on) itself. The identity which is guaranteed by this stability has its origin and its expression in the very act that dissociates Abelard from the incorporated evidence of contradictory desire: his castration. Thus, Abelard's response to Heloise's request for "some sweet semblance" of himself is to hold up this mirror of his castration, to force her to lower her eyes and her sights in genuine, not artful, humility. The text of his letter, in other words, replicates and reapplies to Heloise Fulbert's vengeance, so as to replace an unstable mastery, which is but a pretext and a deceit, with a structure that cannot be overturned from within.

The rest of Abelard's letter treats the question of Heloise's "old perpetual complaint against God," that is, her persistent outrage at the manner in which they have been punished for their offenses. In this closing section, Abelard openly adopts the aim of bringing Heloise to embrace castration—her own as well as his—which she will have to do once her complaint against God has been proved to be unjustified.

Abelard's rebuttal mobilizes a whole arsenal of rhetorical tactics, several of which are consistent with the strategies we have already identified. Throughout the development of his argument, Abelard exhorts Heloise with her own admission that it is still his law and not God's which she fears to offend. That her compliance with his will served only as pretext for the erotic subversion of this law is overlooked, however, in favor of a literalization of both her obedience and his will. By ignoring its ambiguity, Abelard can apply the principle of Heloise's obedience toward a goal which displaces the erotic one. As he approaches his object, he prepares Heloise to accept it: "My praise will never make you proud, but will summon you to higher things, and the more eager you are to please me, the more anxious you will be to embrace what I praise." Further on, he warns her against a dangerous "bitterness of heart" which prevents her from following him and which will eventually cut them off from each other:

> If you are anxious to please me in everything, as you claim, and in this at least would end my torment, or even give me the greatest pleasure, you must rid yourself of it. If it persists you can neither please me nor attain bliss with me. Can you bear me to come to this without you—I whom you declare yourself ready to follow to the very fires of hell? Seek piety in this at least, lest you cut yourself off from me who am hastening, you believe, towards God. [P. 145]

Pleasing Abelard, giving him "the greatest pleasure," attaining bliss with him—it is clearly in those terms that Heloise values her erotic encounters, and this is just as clearly understood by Abelard who, in the sentences we have just cited, makes three direct references to passages from her letters to him (signaled by the attributive formulae "as you claim," "you declare," and "you believe"). In this manner, Abelard implicitly announces his program for the rest of the letter: to dissociate Heloise's submission from its function as mask for the erotic scene and to reinsert it in a stabilized relation to another's will. What this program calls for is a rotation which turns on the pivot of Heloise's subjection, reversing its course from the direction of "the fires of Hell" towards God, to use the theological terms of Abelard's letter.

In the substitution which Abelard proposes, then, the artful abasement of Galatea will give way to a guileless Christian humility. In the process, the selfless will of God is substituted for his own covetous will and thus a purifying obedience to a perfect lord replaces Heloise's abject submission to an unworthy master. This series of substitutions is intricately woven into the fabric of the letter and culminates in a stunning oratorical display summoning Heloise to the service of her new master. This exhortation begins:

> Are you not moved to tears or remorse by the only begotten Son of God who, for you and for all mankind, in his innocence was seized by the hands of impious men, dragged along and scourged, blindfolded, mocked at, buffeted, spat upon, crowned with thorns, finally hanged between thieves on the Cross, at the time so shameful a gibbet, to die a horrible and accursed form of death? [Pp. 150–51]

In this first tableau, Abelard sets up an implicit comparison with his own innocent suffering at "the hands of impious men" which is confirmed by the use of the term "spouse" in the next sentence: "Think of him always, sister, as your true spouse and the spouse of all the Church." This image in turn recalls the opening analogy between the bride of the *Song of Songs* and the monastic woman, a comparison that Abelard justifies to Heloise as "a happy transfer of your married state, for you were previously the wife of a poor mortal and now are raised to the bed of the King of kings" (p. 138). The transfer from a mortal's bed to the sublime embrace of the divine husband is effected by a string of imperatives in which Abelard orders Heloise to the scene of Christ's passion. His rhetoric thus exploits to the limit her obedience while at the same time endeavoring to transfer that obedience to the figure to which he directs her gaze:

Look at him going to be crucified for your sake. . . . Be one of the crowd, one of the women who wept and lamented over him. . . . Have compassion on him . . . look with remorse on him. . . . In your mind be always present at his tomb. . . . Prepare . . . the perfumes for his burial . . . grieve with compassion. . . . See, sister, what great mourning there is. . . . Behold the lamentation and grief. . . . See what right he has over you. [Pp. 151–52]

Having brought her obediently to this point, Abelard then consecrates the transfer by making explicit the comparison we detected at the outset:

It was he who truly loved you, not I. My love, which brought us both to sin, should be called lust, not love. I took my fill of my wretched pleasures in you, and this was the sum total of my love. You say I suffered for you, and perhaps that is true, but it was really through you, and even this, unwillingly; not for love of you but under compulsion, to bring you not salvation but sorrow. But he suffered truly for your salvation, on your behalf of his own free will, and by his suffering, he cures all sickness and removes all suffering. To him, I beseech you, not to me, should be directed all your devotion, all your compassion, all your remorse. [P. 153].

The conversion of Heloise's passion, then, is produced by a displacement of erotic ambiguity onto the Christian symbols and a more-or-less explicit comparison of the earthbound lover, Abelard, with the divine lover, Christ. The comparison has been consistently applied since Abelard's first letter, with his instructions concerning his own death drawn on the model of Christ's passion. We should not overlook the extent to which this type of comparison structured medieval monasticism in general; the monk sought to imitate Christ in his daily life so as to infuse even the most mundane activities with an ordered, transcendent meaning. Abelard's particular exploitation of this topos in his correspondence with Heloise is another means of bringing the erotic experience of disorder into a stabilized relation of opposition with this Christian order, of suppressing the margin between the two that suspends the opposing value within the relation. We have already discussed the major rhetorical devices whereby his text superimposes this conceptual structure on the contradictory logic of Heloise's letters. It remains, however, to analyze briefly in what manner the truth which this structure allows one to posit is the truth of castration.

Abelard's castration inaugurates the order of an adequate representation in which thought, intention, or desire is unequivocally translated by gesture, word, or act. Fulbert's brutal revenge establishes just such a nonarbitrary relation between Abelard's crime and his punishment. The *Historia* relates the event in these terms: "They cut off the parts of my body whereby I had committed the wrong of which they complained" (p. 75). Writing to Heloise, who interprets a divine injustice in this act, he reiterates this relation several times in much the same terms:

> And so it was wholly just and merciful . . . for me to be reduced in that part of my body which was the seat of lust and the sole reason for those desires, so that I could increase in many ways; in order that this member should justly be punished for all its wrongdoings in us, expiate in suffering the sins committed for its amusements, and cut me off from the slough of filth in which I had been wholly immersed in mind as in body. . . . How mercifully did he want me to suffer so much only in that member, the privation of which would also further the salvation of my soul. [P. 148]

In this description, it is not Abelard who is punished or who suffers but "that part of [his] body," "that member." Also, the castration is not represented as a dismemberment, the separation of a whole into its parts, so much as a casting off of a dangerous parasite or the excision of an extraneous, cancerous growth.[26] Fulbert was merely the instrument of the providential healer, the scalpel in the hand of an omniscient surgeon. "By a wound he prevents death, he does not deal it; he thrusts in the steel to cut out the disease. He wounds the body and heals the soul; he makes to live what he should have destroyed, cuts out impurity to leave what is pure" (p. 153).

What is thus cut out and discarded is by its nature improper, that is, without a deeded title to a place in the representable order. Its elimination, therefore, restores the legitimate privilege of proper representation, which need no longer fear the contaminating influence of an imposter in its midst.

> So when divine grace cleansed rather than deprived me of those vile members which from their practice of utmost indecency are called "the parts of shame" and *have no proper name of their own,* what else

did it do but remove a foul imperfection in order to preserve perfect purity? [P. 153]

Suppressing these parts with no proper name, one suppresses as well the need for a deceitful appearance, that is, one which disguises an impropriety.

For Abelard, this conversion of appearances is not limited to his own body, whose purified exterior now adequately reflects the state of his soul. The order of the proper name and the stable system of representation which it guarantees extend to her who had been equally contaminated by the improper. By less violent means, Heloise has also been returned to the fold, and become again a sheep in sheep's clothing. To the crimes for which God has punished them Abelard adds this minor episode:

> You know too how when you were pregnant and I took you to my own country you disguised youself in the sacred habit of a nun, a pretence which was an irreverent mockery of the religion you now profess. Consider, then, how fittingly divine justice, or rather, divine grace brought you against your will to the religion which you did not hesitate to mock, so that you should willingly expiate your profanation in the same habit, and the truth of your reality should remedy the lie of your pretence and correct your falsity. [P. 146]

Where Heloise might see a cruel irony, Abelard considers only the adequate fit of her monastic costume now that it is the "truth of reality" rather than the "lie of pretence." And if we recall the symbolic significance of the nun's habit in the analogy of the black bride, we will see that this corrected truth is her humility, the effacement of her own desire within her husband's domain.

To remedy her falsity, to restore order in the master's house, Heloise need not submit to the painful cure prescribed for Abelard. Her conversion, however, is similarly inscribed in the structure of the proper name:

> Come too, my inseparable companion, and join me in thanksgiving, you who were made my partner both in guilt and in grace. For the Lord is not unmindful also of your own salvation, indeed, he has you much in mind, for by a kind of holy presage of his name he marked you out to be especially his when he named you Heloise, after his own name, Elohim. [P. 149]

Just as the habit Heloise wears is now the sign of a true humility rather than a veiled impropriety, the very name which designates her in the world has been restored to its proper function. Heloise is marked as "especially his" by the name which is first of all not her own. Her entrance into the cloister as the bride of Christ remedies the lie and corrects the falsity whereby she had pretended to that name as her own. Within its walls, the property is turned over to the owner, rehabilitated.

Epilogue

We have isolated what appear to be the most important terms of the exchange between Heloise and Abelard. These letters stage a confrontation between, on the one hand, a system of mirrored oppositions which cloisters the sexual object and, on the other, a generalized economy of desire in which the suspension of such oppositions is the scene of erotic pleasure. Written from within her cloister, Heloise's text dissolves the distinction of inside and outside, the law and its transgression, her vows and her desire. Likewise, the act of negation repeatedly calls up its contrary and maintains Heloise at a constant distance from any effective break with her sexual past. No sign can represent that negation except as a fiction, and in the space of that fiction, the space of one sign and its negated other, the movement of desire is again uncovered, displacing opposition with an unruly difference.

For Abelard, the break which eludes Heloise is to be found in the significance of his castration. Through this healing wound, this punishment which is a grace, this destruction which is a preservation, Abelard has been given a way out of the fiction and into the stable order of the meaningful sign. His mutilation becomes the model of the signifying act, cutting out the pure from the impure so as to represent the proper in its exclusion of the improper. The author of this act is, by definition, the only subject whose discourse does not originate in an other, whose signature on Abelard's body is the mark of a presence uncontaminated by its absent contrary. Singled out in this manner by the hand of God's justice, Abelard is saved not only, as he writes, "from the slough of filth" which is this vile portion of his own body but also, paradoxically, from the contamination of an auto-castration. Although Abelard continually cites "the great

Christian philosopher" Origen, he is careful to distinguish the latter's self-mutilation from his own innocent dismemberment.

> The great Christian philosopher Origen . . . was not afraid to mutilate himself in order to quench completely this fire within him, as if he understood literally the words that those men were truly blessed who castrated themselves for the Kingdom of Heaven's sake [Matt. 19:12], and believed them to be truthfully carrying out the bidding of the Lord about offending members, that we should cut them off and throw them away [Matt. 18:8]. . . . Origen is seriously to be blamed because he sought a remedy for blame in punishment of his body. True, he has zeal for God, but an ill-informed zeal, and the charge of homicide can be proved against him for his self-mutilation. Men think he did this either at the suggestion of the devil or in grave error but, in my case, through God's compassion, it was done by another's hand. I do not incur blame, I escape it. [Pp. 148–49]

Origen's mistake was to believe that his act could signify unequivocally that "zeal for God" which was its motive. Yet, like any other act by which an already compromised subject would attempt to signify its separation from that which contaminates it, this one becomes suspect and serves to confirm, rather than correct, the corruption from the outside. Origen's zeal is finally indissociable from his contempt.

That other great philosopher, Abelard, is protected from even this form of corruption, for the purification he experiences has its source in an undeniably pure, divine subject who alone is entirely present in his acts. Castrated, Abelard is free to become a *man* of God among women, as Origen had done, but without his ambiguous motive. The eunuch, after all, has always been the instrument of "men who wish to keep close watch on their wives": "My present condition removes suspicion of evil-doing so completely from everyone's mind that men who wish to keep close watch on their wives employ eunuchs" (p. 98).[27] The eunuch, in other words, keeps women in their place. As the master's proxy, he functions in a stable opposition to the women of the household and guarantees their exclusion from the masculine domain. Sent by the master, he is the factor of order and the only man in the house whose power remains intact and "above suspicion" when brought into proximity with women.

The masculine prerogative is thus best represented by the man without a sex, for the power conferred by the phallus is in its absence represented by the impotent delegate. Dissociated from the ambiguity of its own potency, the sex of the master, by means of this representation, operates as an unequivocal sign of a legitimate right to power. That that legitimacy collapses when brought into an unmediated proximity with the other sex constitutes Saint Jerome's lament in this passage quoted by Abelard:

> The only fault found in me is my sex, and that only *when Paula comes to Jerusalem.* . . . Before I knew the home of saintly Paula my praises were sung throughout the city, and nearly everyone judged me worthy of the highest office of the church. [P. 98]

This structure of a delegated and thereby legitimized power which is represented and preserved by the eunuch describes, not surprisingly, the situation of the lessons Heloise receives in her second letter from Abelard. In both the analogy of the black bride and the convocation to Christ's passion, Abelard assumes the position of the servant in the master's house, as he has announced in his superscription. His function in that role is not only to guard the door of the cloister but also to represent the master to his bride, to describe the joys of the heavenly bedchamber and the infinite pleasures of the husband's embrace. His function, in other words, is to motivate that other transfer on which depends the system he represents: the transfer of her woman's desire from its human to a divine context. That which the eunuch is powerless to give her, he is, for that very reason, empowered to represent in its pure form: the master-husband as the absent and therefore invulnerable phallus. Metaphorized and transferred, the erotic encounter, through which her subjugation discovers the fiction of its own humility, is projected out of reach, beyond the experience of the world, to where it can do no harm. As white bones, from which the disfiguring flesh has dropped away, Heloise may again enter the chamber with the husband who has preserved her for that moment.

But for Heloise, and for her descendance, the memory of the flesh is powerful.

2 / WRITING ON THE BALCONY
The Portuguese Letters

> We have nothing new to say on the question of these dispositional states. They often, it would seem, grow out of the day-dreams which are so common even in healthy people and to which needlework and similar occupations render women especially prone.
>
> Breuer and Freud, *Studies on Hysteria*

> . . . a woman, seated at her embroidery frame, an insipid task which occupies only the hands, dreams of her lover, while the latter, galloping on the plains with his squadron, is in trouble if he makes a single false move.
>
> Stendhal, *On Love*

 HELOISE'S letters, written from within her cloister, describe a general breakdown of that structure of opposition which alone could allow for a conversion. As we have seen, her text is highly unstable, constantly reversing and passing beyond the meanings it poses. In their mobility, the letters attempt to dodge the immobilizing terms that Abelard has placed on their experience and, at least for a moment, to break a silence. This deconstruction of stable meaning is the activity which threatens the edifice Abelard has built and in which he has enclosed, along with Heloise, his unruly past. For this reason, the correspondence continues after a certain point only with answers to questions about monastic rule. The limit placed on their exchange is set at the barrier that defines Heloise's claustration, so that by drawing the line Abelard can proceed to reconstruct the walls behind which she agrees (in ambiguous terms, it is true) to remain. The cloister, in this manner, exists not only as the physical site of a woman's enclosure, but also as a bar to a disruptive practice of the language. As Abelard's analogy of the black bride illustrates, the cloistering of the woman, by removing her from circulation in a public domain, sets up a freely mobile masculine desire as the noncontradictory self-referential source of meaningful distinction. On the other hand, the movement of Galatea, her flight into the willows, suspends the very possibility of such distinctions between outside and inside, seen and unseen, and, ject and object of the flight. It raises the question w repeatedly puts to her lover, the question of preced follows whom.

At stake in the exchange between Heloise and Abelard, then, is the possibility of stable meaning and the proper functioning of structural oppositions. By breaking the silence of the cloister, Heloise uncovers a puzzling zone of indeterminacy which is covered over again only when she agrees to return to the cloister. In that indeterminate space, the discourse of the master encounters another image of its own mastery and stability.

This movement into the no man's land between feminine closure and masculine mobility will take us now to a text that has often been compared to the letters of Heloise and Abelard: *The Portuguese Letters*.[1] Such comparisons, however, leave us with an even more obvious distinction between the two texts: while Heloise writes in a dialogue with the letters from Abelard, Mariana's letters are punctuated only by the silence of her lover. That this absence of the other's response could nevertheless lead Mariana outside the closure of her own cloistered discourse is one reason why, before reading those letters, we will consider another example of the power of a woman's speech. It comes from the literature of psychoanalysis.

It was the idea that by understanding the nature of a disorder one could learn more about the proper functioning of a mechanism which led Freud, in the 1890s, to concentrate on the study of neurotics in order to refine the model of the human psyche. During this period, he published his various studies on hysteria. It is to these earliest theoretical writings and case histories of hysterical women that historians of psychoanalysis—beginning with Freud himself—have turned to isolate the first appearances of what were to become the fundamental discoveries of that science. After the turn of the century, while these concepts were being developed, Freud's publications only rarely speculated on specifically feminine-inflected structures, and it was not until after 1920 that the Oedipal scenario was worked out in any detail in relation to women. In this interval, many of the troubling implications of understanding hysteria would be deferred, so that even as late as 1931 Freud would readily concede that psychoanalysis had not progressed beyond the prehistory of feminine sexuality.[2] This confessed inadequacy has tended to obscure the fact that, during the period of its own prehistory, psychoanalysis was centrally concerned with the question of what women want.

In the first stage of the investigation of hysteria, Freud and his collaborator, Josef Breuer, attempted to explain the onset of this disorder with the neurophysiological model. In this account, the hysterical symptom was the sign of a psychic defense against the onslaught of organic changes during puberty. As Freud, however, began to interview more and more hysterics (Breuer, in circumstances I will discuss, having given up their collaboration), he discovered that the great majority of them had similar stories to tell once they could be led to recall their earliest childhood: a story of seduction or even rape by the father, or a fatherlike figure. This in turn led Freud to adopt the theory of the etiology of hysteria: at an age before she could react with understanding, the hysteric had been the victim of a sexual attack or attempted seduction. The event, in its most minute particulars, was stored in the memory until, at puberty, when its significance could be assessed and the correct conscious associations made with what had been learned of sexual behavior, the memory attempted to find its way into the active reminiscences and was blocked.

It is only at this point that the hysterical symptom is formed by means of the process Breuer and Freud agreed to call conversion. Because the memory is denied the path into consciousness which would lead through a chain of unpleasant associations, the powerful affective charge which is attached to it cannot be abreacted, or, if one prefers, dealt with and thereby diminished. As this process of abreaction, of placing a particular thought or memory in the associative chain of coded values and meanings common to all members of society, is short-circuited, the associations are forced to occur elsewhere. The hysterical symptom breaks out in a physical complaint for which no organic cause is present. The specific form the symptom takes is thus always contingent on some detail from the repressed seduction scene: for example, a throbbing pain or numbness in some part of the body which the seducer had touched. The hysteric thereby strikes a compromise with the offending remembrance: it is to remain outside her consciousness, the agency whereby she functions as an accepted member of society as represented by its codes, but it will be given total control over her body.

Whereas this theory of hysterical symptom-formation and its treatment only needed refinement as Freud gained more experience of hysteria, he was not long in detecting the basic error in his trauma or seduction theory. In 1897, two years after the publication of *Studies on Hysteria*, Freud began to suspect that the memory of the specific event was frequently masked by several layers of fantasy which had to be identified as such and penetrated before one could arrive at the truth of the trauma. This process of a progressive dismantling of fictions was made more difficult by the lack of any mark distinguishing the fantasized recollection from the true memory. As Freud wrote to Wilhelm Fliess, "there is no 'indication of reality' in the unconscious, so that it is impossible to distinguish between truth and emotionally-charged fiction."[3] Freud held to the view for several months that the fantasies were defensive formations which decoyed conscious remembering away from an awful truth, but, in September 1897, he confessed to Fliess what he had finally admitted to himself: "Let me tell you straight away the great secret which has been slowly dawning on me in recent months. I no longer believe in my *neurotica*."[4] In other words, Freud was forced to dispense with his theory of a real seduction and to consider the implications of the hysteric's total invention of such an "event."

The major implication—and the reason Freud delayed for several years publishing a retraction of the trauma theory—was the sexualization of childhood and even infancy, through recognition of which psychoanalysis broke from its parent disciplines of psychology and neurology. Among the latter effects of this revolution, one can read the whole of what has come to be the theory and practice of Freudian analysis. But we are interested here in more localized implications of this shift, the implications for the analysis of hysteria, which tend to become lost in Freud's eagerness to get on to the problems of little boys.[5]

What gives the hysterical fantasy its specific structure is the use of the passive voice as a fictional device to hide an active desire. In order to read the material with accuracy, the subject—object, seducer—seduced syntax must be reversed: for "I was violated" one reads "I (wished to) violate." The guilt which would result were the wish given access to consciousness has at least three supports: (1) the guilt that attaches to a forbidden desire for the father; (2) the guilt that attaches to the false accusation of the father; (3) the guilt associated, for the girl, with an active pursuit of a desired object. This third possibility necessitates the recourse to the duplicity of the passive voice, which is the reversal mechanism of the fantasy and which makes it at least partially acceptable to conscious memory.

Freud's discovery of the hysteric's duplicity occurred at about the midpoint of his self-analysis as recorded in his correspondence with Fliess. As the editor of the translated edition points out, the two investigations had a dynamic relation to each other, the former giving Freud insight into his own Oedipal scenario (what he called his hysteria) and the latter, the first intimations of the Oedipus complex, giving him a different means of approach to the hysteric's complaint.[6] The validity of the Oedipal model began finding constant affirmation in successful analyses, with one result being that Freud's caseload—which in 1897 was so low that he started taking on patients free of charge—increased steadily, to the point that a year later, in October 1898, he could report his daily exhaustion from "an avalanche of patients," half of whom, he notes, were now men.[7] The technique, which would emerge only later, sought to bring the Oedipal material into conscious view so as to move toward a resolution that compensated the renunciation of the mother with an opening onto the whole field of legitimate sexual activity. The motor of this displacement had to be an identification with the father as active sexual partner, an identification which entailed renouncing—repressing—the child's passivity in the sexual encounter with the mother.

When, a number of years later, Freud attempted to specify the pertinent differences between the male and female passages through the Oedipal stage, he alternated between, on the one hand, insisting on a single model for both sexes (the phallic phase), so as not to discard too early the universal entry into the conflict, and, on the other, the necessity of explaining the contrast in the forms of emergence from the conflict: the fact that the little boy exits wanting to be like the father—with the important exception of his choice of mate—and the little girl exits wanting to have a baby. Luce Irigaray has shown how, in order to arrive at this distinction, Freud had to invert his procedure in the case of the feminine model, working backwards from the norm of female sexuality and positing various transformations or shifts within the triangular structure which could produce the (desired) result.[8] But as another result, the model of the feminine Oedipus has no internal consistency, and the genetic logic of Freud's argument has to be forced. The only thread holding it together is the prior knowledge of where it has to lead.

It would appear that, like Freud perhaps, we have let ourselves be lured away from the question of hysteria by the not-so-tragic mask of Oedipus. But the detour may have been necessary to put us back on our course by reminding us that, while Oedipus lives out a long and relatively fruitful life in a spirit of contrition, his daughter Antigone must choose between an early death and a humiliating submission to the state.[9] The early investigations of hysteria brought Freud very close to a realization that would be overshadowed by the happy insight of Oedipus and then denied when, later, he attempted to extend Oedipal causality to matters female.

Simply put, the hysteric's symptomatically convulsed and contorted body states eloquently the lack of any acceptable resolution for the conflict between active sexual impulses and the coded laws of the society into which she must insert herself. While, like her brothers, she has to move out of the enclosing duality with her mother and make room for a third party, this move towards socialization halts at the limits which define the family unit. Nor can the renunciation of the mother be compensated by a shift from a passive to an active position in the syntax of seduction. The active subject of the discourse of desire—represented by the father—cannot be made available to the girl-child through identification if the socialization process is to go forward only as far as expected. Thus, the girl's entry into a larger social network is as the object of another's discourse. The position of active subject of the transitive verb is barred by the structure of the father's law, which Catherine Clément discerns as follows: "Women must circulate and must not cause to circulate [*La femme doit circuler et non pas faire circuler*]."[10] Feminine culpability is the inevitable support of this circulation order, since a transgression of the passive, intransitive female position if structurally homologous to a transgression of the incest prohibition, and therefore the grounds for that culpability can shift: to desire the father or to desire *like* the father are mutually reinforcing of the feminine exclusion. Coming to terms with this double injunction, or rather accepting the terms of silence it imposes, distinguishes the production of the feminine from that of the masculine, for in the latter process desiring the father and desiring like the father exclude rather than reinforce each other. Thus, the boy-child has a choice, although to be properly masculine he must make the right choice. This is to state in revised form what we have already implied: the social code compensates the boy for the repression of the first source of sexual pleasure with the offer of another form of sexual activity, while the analogous process of feminization demands the repression of the original pleasure even as it bars access to the pleasure sought by "masculine" desire.

This analysis of the fundamentally hysterical character of the feminine norm is the inadvertent byproduct of Freud's investigation into its more pathological manifestations. Even from within the context of our general suspicion of this norm, we can still understand this work, conducted in quite a different context, as asking the question of why some women are more hysterical than others. In the course of his long association with hysterics, Freud revised his answer to that question several times, until in 1909, in one of his last essays on the subject, he wrote:

> One may often observe that it is just those girls who in the years before puberty showed a boyish character and inclinations who tend to become hysterical at puberty. In whole series of cases the hysterical neurosis is nothing but an excessive overaccentuation of the typical wave of repression through which the masculine type of sexuality is removed and the woman emerges.[11]

Hysterics, in other words, are girls who must work extra hard to become women because their "boyish character and inclinations" have been allowed to develop unchecked for too long.

The hysterical symptom as solution is ambiguous on more than one level. First of all, as a sign, it is constructed out of the confrontation between, on the one hand, the impulse to signify desire, to assume a place in the social network which is a function of that desire, and, on the other hand, the powerful exclusion which blocks that place. Second, therefore, the hysteric comes to occupy a position midway between the masculine and feminine insertion into the symbolic register of social exchange. The conscious negation of what Freud termed the "masculine type of sexuality" secures her status as a circulated object, while at the same time the physical symptom is a mute sign of her activity as a cause of that circulation. To Freud's famous observation that "hysterics suffer mainly from reminiscences," one would have to add that their reminiscences cause them to suffer precisely to the extent that the doors leading out of the stifling family triangle of their past and into the register of symbolic activity are marked "Men only."

While Freud's theoretical conclusion concerning hysteria stopped considerably short of any questioning of the active/passive distinction, the descriptions of his analytic technique, which emerged almost directly from his early treatment of hysterics, repeatedly confirm the implications that have been drawn. Already in the first case reported in any detail in the *Studies on Hysteria*, that of the pseudonymous Anna O., which was conducted by Breuer, the discovery was made which was to determine the whole course of psychoanalytic therapy: that the most reliable antidote or cure for the hysterical symptom was talking. Indeed, Breuer did not come to the case of Anna's hysteria with any prior understanding of the worth of the method, which he called "cathartic." It was entirely Anna's invention of her own speech, which she called "the talking cure"—in English since one of her symptoms was the loss of her ability to use or understand German—that led gradually to the identification and the conscious recall of the events signified by various symptoms. Once spoken, the symptom evaporated, as the memory no longer required an hysterical conversion in order to signify itself.

As Freud took over the method Breuer had stumbled upon, he systematically eliminated all of the extraneous elements to the "talking cure" which were holdovers from earlier techniques: hypnosis, hydrotherapy, electrotherapy, and so on. He also promoted to a principle of his technique Anna's assurance in leading the way to her own recovery, following a course which Breuer had considered particularly inefficient as it took in far more than the limited symptomatic behavior. In his introduction to the case of Dora, Freud explains the reason for this partial abdication of the physician's control:

> [At the time of the publication of *Studies on Hysteria*] the work of analysis started out from the symptoms, and aimed at clearing them up one after the other. Since then I have abandoned that technique, because I found it totally inadequate for dealing with the finer structure of neurosis. I now let the patient himself choose the subject of the day's work, and in that way I start out from whatever surface his unconscious happens to be presenting to his notice at the moment.[12]

All of his other refinements of the technique were aimed at forcing the neurotic into the position of conscious subject of his / her own discourse, which meant, in the case of an hysteric, permitting the unconscious wish to signify desire to come to consciousness by defeating a measure of the repression that detoured it into a physical symptom. Dora's recovery, for example, lay along the path of the conscious realization of her desire for Herr K., and behind that, for Frau K., a realization which had been effectively blocked by her fantasy of Herr K.'s sexual aggression toward her.[13]

This formulaic description of hysteria's cure cannot, however, disguise its significant limitations. If at the source of the disorder is the process of normal feminization, that process whereby the girl-child exchanges the sexual scene of infancy for the guilty scene of adult sexuality, then, despite Freud's open-minded attention to the field beyond the specific symptom, the theory which does not question this process cannot yield anything but a technique for treating symptoms. This is very nearly the conclusion reached by Breuer and Freud at the end of their first theoretical paper on hysteria, where they concede a most significant limitation on their treatment: "It is of course true that we do not cure hysteria *in so far as it is a matter of disposition*."[14] Insofar, in other words, as little girls persist in growing up with a "boyish character and inclinations."

In a sense, the treatment of hysteria cannot move beyond its earliest and most spectacular failure, the case of Anna O. This failure is not recorded by Breuer, whose case history implies that he conducted the cure to a complete success. In fact, Anna did eventually recover more or less, but only after Breuer had precipitously dropped her case. When Freud discussed the incident almost thirty years later in his "On the History of the Psychoanalytic Movement," he attributed his colleague's gradual loss of interest in their collaboration to what happened the last time Breuer visited Anna. The details are recorded in Jones's biography.[15] It appears that after announcing to the girl and her family that the treatment had effectively run its course, Breuer was suddenly called back to Anna's bedside, where he found her in the last throes of hysterical pregnancy. His former patient let him know in no uncertain terms that the child she was laboring to produce was his. Breuer, of course, could not have anticipated these effects of the process which would later become known as transference. It seems that he could not bear the spectacle of such monstrous language from a woman of Anna's education and that he felt in some oblique way responsible for her degradation. On the other hand, perhaps he saw in that moment the powerful force unleashed by the "talking cure" and feared that its violence could not be spent until it had upset every notion of decorum and propriety.

Freud was at the same time less frightened by what Breuer called the hysteric's "private theatre" and more determined that it should not get out of hand. His treatment, after all, as he frequently told his *neurotica*, could not be expected to produce a miracle reordering of the circumstances of their lives, the circumstances which the analysis revealed as lying at the source of their illness. The *Studies on Hysteria* concludes with this exchange between Freud and his patients:

> I have often been faced by this objection: "Why, you tell me yourself that my illness is probably connected with my circumstances and the events of my life. You cannot alter these in any way. How do you propose to help me then?" And I have been able to make this reply: "No doubt fate would find it easier than I do to relieve you of

your illness. But you will be able to convince yourself that much will be gained if we succeed in transforming your hysterical misery into common unhappiness. With a mental life that has been restored to health you will be better armed against that unhappiness."[16]

The powers of the analyst are not to be compared with those of an all-knowing fate. The former can content himself with bringing patients under his care to accept the chance limitations on their happiness and to renounce the futile rebellion of their bodies. While giving the hysteric the means to translate her mute symptom into the common language, analysis nonetheless risks becoming an agent of censure, helpless as it is to change the circumstances of a woman's life. The course of the treatment therefore also risks describing a circle, for at its end is the redis-covery of the enforced silence and inactivity to which the hys-teric's body had refused its submission. In the course of its trajectory, the analysis will have operated a displacement: "to suffer, as always and in all cases, but this time out of guilt instead of suffering physically without knowing why."[17] Knowing her guilt, the former hysteric will be less *disposed* to break the silence.

In suggesting above that the treatment of hysteria could not move beyond its first failure, I was thinking of the case of Dora. The analyses were separated by about seventeen years, during which time Freud had totally revised his theory of hysteria and its treatment in view of the discovery of sexuality's role in the neurotic formation. It was this discovery that so disturbed Breuer, causing him to retreat in haste from Anna's cure and giving Freud his first evidence of the mechanism of transference. It is then significant that Dora's analysis, which, unlike Anna's, was conducted in full cognizance of the sexual material, broke down in almost the same circumstances as the earlier one. Freud, in his postscript to the case history, attributes Dora's premature decision to end her treatment to the process of transference, which he had neglected to recognize and thus, as he puts it, failed to master in good time.[18] There are, no doubt, many possible contingent explanations for this oversight, some of which Freud discusses. We might wonder, however, if the lapse does not point to the continued dismissal of a woman's discourse even within the context of its therapeutic retrieval. Did Freud, in other words, share Breuer's motive for—if not his reaction to—

the failure to anticipate his own objectification within the dynamic of Dora's desire?

But there is still another way to read the final scene in Dora's drama. It is to imagine that, even if Freud could not understand the language of her transference until too late, Dora knew all too well what was coming. She timed her exit from the professor's life to rob him of the exquisite pleasure of turning her into the perfect closed circle of the successful analysis, forcing him to preface his case history with repeated disclaimers as to its adequacy for the understanding of hysteria. Knowing what was coming, Dora decided not to wait until the doctor took yet another one of her productions, dismantled it, and left her "a common unhappiness." From Freud's perspective, such a refusal of the health his treatment might have restored for the pleasure of a petty revenge is the clearest sign of a continued pathology. For Dora, however, might not a few physical tics represent a small price to pay for her escape from the promised cure? After all, it is possible that Dora's relapse was only secondarily the revenge that Freud, in his disappointment, took it to be. What he terms her "flight from life into disease" may have had as its propelling force a desire which, in order to reverse its direction, would have had to renounce all activity.

One could object that Dora's protest was an exercise in futility, ending as it did in another ambiguous symptom which left intact the fundamental exclusion of her discourse from the common language.[19] Clément, for example, places an important reservation on the effect of the hysteric's contestation:

> It's true, hysteria upsets and disturbs the family . . . but very little in comparison with the passage into action which is writing, political action, the passage into inscription in the symbolic. This is not the case with Dora for one cannot say that the fact of her passage to posterity through Freud's text and even Freud's failure is a symbolic act. . . . The distinction between those who properly fulfill their function of protest, even with all possible violence (but which is afterwards closed off again), and those who arrive at symbolic inscription by whatever means they get there seems essential to me. To create scandalous scenes, to throw fits, to upset the relations within the family, all of that can be closed off again.[20]

It is true that Dora's voice is never heard again. Her protest, if that is what it was, is only an echo in Freud's text, her name the title, not the signature. Even that name is not hers but one Freud lends his character to protect his former patient. The woman he calls Dora is thus put into circulation as the object of a clinical exercise without the risk that she might be called to account as the subject of these sordid confessions. These pages are a testament, finally, to Dora's silence.[21]

If, therefore, we are looking for such an inscription of the posthysterical subject in the symbolic order, an inscription which would modify the fundamental exclusion of that act, it will have to be elsewhere. Dora, however, and the other characters in Freud's hysterical plots, will at least have given us an idea of where to look. What if one of them had left a written account of her passage out of a closed hysterical silence? As a record of this passage, the account would have to substitute for the conventions of the case history the conventions of autobiography, so that to imagine such a text is to imagine the interlocutor as the silent pole through which passes the invention of the writing subject. The analytical scene would, in a sense, return to its point of departure with Anna's discovery of "the talking cure" but displace Breuer's intervening narrative point of view. Such a text, therefore, would have to renounce the gallant protection of the cloak of pseudonymity, the borrowed name bestowed by a man, and agree to disclose its scandalous activity.

For an idea of what such a text could be, has been, we can read the five letters which a woman who calls herself Mariana wrote to her unnamed lover. The letters have been published for more than three hundred years with the title *Letters from a Portuguese Nun* or, simply, *The Portuguese Letters*.[22]

Mariana, a nun in a Portuguese convent, has had a brief affair with an officer in the French forces which occupied Portugal in the 1660s. The seduction seems to have proceeded in a Don Juanesque fashion, with assurances of unending devotion and hints of a respectable conjugal future. With Portugal safely secured to the French alliance, however, the *chevalier* has been called back to France, leaving his erotic conquest behind with only a few vague promises of a return. It is shortly after this departure that the first letter is written.

The first image with which this letter names the loss is that of the lover's eyes:

> Can it be true that this absence, for which my suffering, although it is very ingenious, cannot find a name sinister enough, will deprive me forever of looking into those eyes where I saw so much love, and which allowed me to experience feelings [mouvements] that filled me with joy, which took the place of everything else and which, finally, were all I needed [me suffisaient]? Alas! Mine are deprived of the only light that gave them life, they have nothing left but tears.[23]

The lover's eyes, as the source of light, joy, love, mouvements, in short, "everything else," focus the loss just as they provided Mariana with her brief experience of suffisance. This adequacy of visual reflection from eye to eye—from source of light to mirror and back again—is closed upon itself in a silent exchange. The nostalgia for that moment of the unbroken circle is marked in the inadequacy of the exchange that takes it place—through words which always fall short.

The visual relation, through which one glimpses directly the spontaneous mouvements of passion, has given way, then, to the tenuous linking provided by the letter.[24] At the beginning of this correspondence, the letter attempts through its allegorical rhetoric to resurrect the body's own power to signify. Love, pain, sighs, ill-fortune, and heart are all personified as message-senders:

> A thousand times a day, I send my sighs toward you, they seek you out everywhere, and, as my own reward for so much anxiety, they bring me back the same brutally honest message as my ill-fortune, which in its cruelty cannot bear me to flatter myself, and which tells me at every moment: "Cease, unfortunate Mariana, cease consuming yourself vainly looking for a lover whom you will never see again. . . ." Your last letter reduced my heart to a bizarre state; it felt such powerful agitations [mouvements] that it seemed to want to separate itself from me in order to go find you. [Pp. 39–40]

Mouvements, then, find their linguistic translation in a rhetoric of personification by means of which Mariana signifies herself as a loose conglomerate of symbolizing impulses whose unifying principle—the lover's eyes—is absent.

> I was so overcome by all those violent emotions that I remained
> unconscious more than three hours. . . . Since these events, I have
> been indisposed many times, but how can I ever be free of such
> complaints as long as I must go without seeing you? [P. 40]

The figures correspond to the body's uncontrolled production of
the symbols of its shattered unity—the symptomatic language of
the trauma.

In this first letter, as in the next, Mariana's discourse remains
caught in the paradox of its nostalgia for the silent adequacy of
lover and beloved. So as to see herself once again as the object of
her lover's gaze, she welcomes her current suffering at least
insofar as it gives her proof of her continued subjection: "It
seems to me that I am fond of those miseries of which you are the
sole cause" (p. 39); "I understand [these misfortunes] without
complaint because they come from you" (p. 40); "I do not want to
nurture a hope which would surely give me some pleasure and I
want to be sensitive only to pain." The first letter ends with the
formulation of a demand in which Mariana reclaims her position
as object, as passive victim of the other's acts: "Adieu, I cannot
write any more. Adieu, love me forever and make me suffer still
more pain" (p. 42).

Mariana cannot give up the letter writing and return to the
previous accord of the lover's silent correspondence because the
fact of writing has altered irrevocably the significance of that
silence. By breaking the silence, her letters disturb the reflection
and reveal cracks in the mirror. The more she writes, the more
she reads in her lover's continued lack of response a declaration
which accuses the very notion of *suffisance*:

> It seems to me that I am doing the greatest possible disservice to
> my heart's feelings in trying to communicate them to you in writ-
> ing. How happy I would be if you could measure them through
> comparison with the violence of your own! But I must not leave it
> to you [*me rapporter à vous*—more literally, refer myself to you]. [P.
> 43]

In the absence of an assured redundancy, the letter is forced to
pursue an exploration of the gap and thereby to widen, rather
than close, the distance which separates Mariana and her lover.

> Shall I never see you again here in my room, with all the passion
> and frenzy that you used to display? But alas, I am deluding myself
> and I know only too well that all the feelings [*mouvements*] that
> stirred my heart and mind were for you only the products of a
> fleeting pleasure and they passed as soon as that pleasure ceased.
> [P. 44]

Thus do the letters, these poor substitutes for a transparent
relation, destroy little by little that which can only be recovered
as a delusion, a fiction.

The third letter opens by addressing two questions to this
abyss: "What will become of me and what would you have me
do?" (p. 47). The articulation of the question of the other's desire
no longer operates a closure, for an excess is produced which
cannot be dissociated from the fact of the articulation itself.
While the first letter calculated that articulation as a loss, in this
letter it functions as a surplus which comes to fill in the void
discovered by the question of the self. In effect, the third letter
marks stages in the birth of the writing subject.

It is in the first lines of this letter that Mariana announces her
project of a cure, for which purpose she must adopt both positions in a dialogue of confrontation:

> I had even contemplated several half-hearted projects whereby I
> would concentrate all my efforts on curing myself. . . . Yet having
> finally only myself to combat, I could never have foreseen all my
> weaknesses nor anticipated everything that I now suffer. [P. 47]

As if to demonstrate this combat, the letter proceeds to trace a
circle of reversals which represent skirmishes in Mariana's battle
with herself: first, the fear of the lover's indifference, then anger
at the certain signs of that indifference, followed by regret that
the man she loves cannot experience her exquisite pain, horror at
the thought that she has wished such suffering on him, and,
finally, gratitude that, through his indifference, he has been
spared her misery. In the course of that spiral, Mariana writes: "I
know neither who I am, not what I am doing, nor what I want. I
am torn by a thousand conflicting feelings. Can anyone imagine
a more deplorable state?" (p. 48). Mariana pauses briefly for this
overview before plunging back into the fray, and in the space

defined by that triple unknown, the question with which the letter began has been reformulated as a statement.

To this series of unknowns, Mariana adds a fourth, which, like the others, is thrown up in the midst of a circular movement of contradictions. "I do not know why I write to you," she writes (p. 49). From this point on, the project of the cure is taken over by the process of losing her ignorance about why she writes. Beginning with the third letter, then, it is the relationship to her own discourse about her desire which counteracts and displaces the suffering in her relationship to her lover.

Although the effects of this displacement are most evident in the final two letters, the crucial third letter acts as a pivot in Mariana's eradication of silence and ignorance through writing. For example, she makes the discovery of a discrepancy in her own text which she equates with the *mauvaise foi* of her lover:

> It seems to me that I can be little pleased with either my grief or the excess of my love . . . I live, faithless creature that I am and I do just as many things to preserve my life as to give it up. Oh! it shames me to death—is my despair then only in my letters? If I loved you as much as I have said a thousand times I do, why have I not already died long ago? I have deceived you and it is your turn to reproach me. [P. 49]

Even as she recognizes the hyperbolic cast of her rhetoric, that excess of her love which is only in her letters, Mariana is seemingly unable to renounce the comfort it affords, for she includes the exclamation "It shames me to death [*j'en meurs de honte*]." Yet with the recognition she has already come very close to this statement in the next letter, where the effect of the displacement is unmistakable: "I write more for myself than for you; I am only trying to comfort myself" (p. 58). Indeed, the letters, as the sole locus of the hyperbolic figure "dying for love," are themselves one of those "things" Mariana does to preserve her life.

The third letter is in this respect exemplary, for it contains no reference to the sort of physical disruptions that interfered with the act of writing the first two, bringing each of them to an abrupt close—letter 1: "Adieu, I cannot write any more" (p. 42); letter 2: "Your poor Mariana cannot write any more. She feels faint as she finishes this letter" (p. 46). Instead, the third letter is punctuated by the hyperbole of death, that is, a figure which has a rhetorical rather than a physical force. "This thought kills me and I am frightened to death that you were never deeply touched by any of our pleasures" (pp. 47–48). Toward the end of the letter, this figure assumes the form of a fantasized rehabilitation of that perfect correspondence, in silence, between the two lovers:

> Treat me mercilessly! . . . Write me that you want me to die of love for you! . . . A tragic end would force you no doubt to think of me often, you would treasure my memory and perhaps you would be deeply moved by my sudden death. . . . Adieu, promise me that you will miss me tenderly if I die of grief. [P. 49–50]

The letter, however, refuses to end there. The melodramatic vision of "a tragic end" cannot cancel out the obscure sense which Mariana has just acquired of a break within the first-person subject of her letters. The relationship between her despair and the letters she writes exceeds the limits of a representational schema through the fictional possibilities of her own discourse. Mariana is forced to confront the notion that, as she writes, she is producing rather than merely registering the events of a subjectivity.

> Adieu, I wish that I had never met you. Ah! I sense keenly the falsity of that sentiment and I know, as I am writing to you, that I prefer to be miserable in my love for you than to have never met you at all. [P. 50]

Once again, Mariana has become a reader of her text and as she does so she superimposes two versions of her seduction: the first, which has prevailed until now, is the melodramatic vision of her victimization; the second, which has yet to be explored, accords a place to her active desire. The second version only appears through the foregrounding of the writing subject and the momentary awareness of its active inscription. That is, it is only to the extent that Mariana affirms the break between the subject of the letters and the imaginary self-presence of silence, of death, that a move beyond the static closure of her victimization fantasy will become possible.

It is with the announcement of such a move that the third letter ends. Unlike the first two letters, where physical symptoms take over the signifying process and force the writing to a close, the third text resists the censuring agency. "My letters to you are too long; I am not very considerate of you and I ask your forgiveness. . . . It seems to me that I tell you far too often how intolerable my situation is" (p. 50). Still reading what she writes, Mariana moves to moderate that exaggeration, affirming as she does so the desire that has erupted within her silence and the language it has given her:

> Yet, I thank you from the bottom of my heart for the despair which you caused me, and I detest the tranquillity in which I lived before I knew you. Adieu, my passion grows with every minute. Oh! how many things I have to say to you!

With that final proleptic phrase, Mariana is inscribed as/ inscribes all the possibilities of the language that her tranquillity denied. It is at the same time the announcement and the realization of the passage *outside*.

The fourth letter, the longest in the series, is also the first to use a paragraph break. This formal interruption is emblematic of a more important breakthrough, however, since this letter provides the scene for the reenactment of the memory which is at the origin of Mariana's "intolerable state." The breakthrough has indeed already occurred, for what is reenacted and recalled is a passage outside tranquillity's walls. Our epigraph from Stendhal, with its opposition of insipid domesticity and hazardous exteriority, sets the stage for this passage and for the scene of Mariana's seduction by her *chevalier*-lover. As she recalls that moment, however, her place in the action becomes ambiguous:

> Dona Brites has been after me these last few days to leave my room and, thinking to distract me, she took me for a walk on the balcony which looks out over the town of Mertola. I followed her, and was struck right away by a painful memory which made me cry the rest of the day. . . . She brought me back in and I threw myself on the bed. . . . I often saw you pass that spot with a charming air, and I was on the balcony that fatal day when I began to feel the first effects of my unfortunate passion. It seemed to me that you wanted to please me, although you did not know me. I convinced myself that you had noticed me among all of those who were with me. I imagined to myself that, when you stopped, you wanted me to see you better so that I might admire the skill and grace with which you handled your horse. I was seized by fear when you took him over a difficult spot. In a word, I took a secret interest in all your actions. I

felt that you yourself were not indifferent to me and I understood everything you did to be for me. [P. 55]

Mariana's memory is brought into focus when she leaves her cell and passes outside the walls of the convent. Her resistance to such a move, which is signaled here, has already been noted in the second letter: "I leave my room as little as possible, this room where you came so often to see me" (p. 46). Once on the balcony—a neither-here-nor-there space which hangs between the convent and the world outside—she is "struck by a painful memory" of an earlier occasion when she had stood in the same place and looked out at the distance. Back in her room, the details of the scene arrange themselves on the page, where Mariana's syntax folds back on itself several times: "I often saw you. . . . It seemed to me that you wanted to please me. . . . I convinced myself that you had noticed me. . . . I imagined to myself that . . . you wanted me to see you better. . . ." The imaginary dimension of these events produces a reversal within the subject/object relation so as to hide Mariana's activity of observation and, behind that, the "first effects" of her desire. The text, however, betrays that imaginary mechanism whereby all activity and all risk is shifted onto the horseman. The desire that brings Mariana out onto the balcony also takes her beyond its narrow limits into the domain of the horseman, for, as she writes, "I took a secret interest in all your actions. . . . I understood everything you did to be for me." That is: *Je prenais pour moi tout ce que vous faisiez*, which also translates as "I took everything you did for myself." By means of that double-entendre, Mariana's text signals the desire to speak from the position of the horseman, to take its chances in the world outside the quiet cloister.

Retrieving that desire from beneath the screen of the opposing fantasy of her passive victimization has been the work of these letters. In the process, the letter itself has become the vehicle of the passage out of the cloister. Like her *chevalier*, Mariana pushes it forward with a skill and a grace, riding/writing her way over the dangerous obstacles in her path. It is a process, then, of taking back her word, of breaking her promise of silence:

> I should not write this to you . . . I am often convinced that I should not demonstrate so violently feelings which you disavow. For a

long time now an officer has been waiting for this letter. I had resolved to write in such a way that you would receive my letter without disgust. But it is too extravagant. I must finish it. Alas! It is not in my power to bring myself to do so. . . . It is true that I should not write to you about a love that displeases you. . . . I am starting over again and the officer will leave. What does it matter if he leaves; I am writing more for myself than for you. I am only trying to comfort myself. And thus, the length of my letter will frighten you so that you will not read it. [Pp. 55, 57–58]

That Mariana might frighten her lover by her letters, by the exercise of unbridled, violent love, returns us once more to the remembered scene. In this reprise, the man on horseback has (been) ridden off and the woman is writing on the balcony.

The fifth and last letter consolidates the breakthrough of the preceding two. Its six paragraphs of varying lengths signal the greater control exercised over the structure. As Mariana is writing to take leave of her lover, her first concern is to establish the finality of this act of writing to him. It is an intent which can only be realized by the intervention of a third person, to whom Mariana defers the task of writing the other's name:

I am writing to you for the last time. . . . At the first opportunity, I will send you everything I still have of yours. Do not fear that I will write to you. I will not even put your name on the package. I have asked Dona Brites to take care of all of that for me. [P. 63]

Before she ends this letter, Mariana will be tempted to retract her decision so as to demonstrate with a future letter the anticipated success of her self-administered cure. But, in a final reversal, she ends as she began: "I will not write to you again" (p. 69).

Between the terms of this repetition, the letter conducts an analytic review of the case that restores the context of Mariana's encounter with her *chevalier*. Had not each of them been taken in by a mirage promising uninterrupted self-satisfaction, *suffisance*?

I understand that, ordinarily, a nun is hardly well-suited for love. Yet, if one could be reasonable about such things, one would do better to set one's sights on her rather than on other women for there is nothing to prevent her from dwelling continually on her love. She is not distracted by the thousand little things that enter-

tain and occupy women of the world. It occurs to me that it cannot
be very pleasant to see one's mistress always preoccupied with
trivial things. [Pp. 64–65]

Thus, it is not hard to imagine how a man of the world, wishing
for once to inspire a single-minded passion, might find his
interests best served in a convent.

There are limits, however, on whatever credit he might have
thought was his due. The limits are those which have been
placed on Mariana's worth.

> I cannot deny that you have the advantage over me and that you
> inspired in me a passion that caused me to lose my mind. But there
> is little cause for you to boast: I was young and credulous. I have
> been closed up in this convent since childhood. The only men I had
> ever seen were unattractive and I had never received the sort of
> flattery which you lavished on me. It seemed to me that the beauty
> you found in me and that you gave me to see was not mine but a
> debt I owed you [il me semblait que je vous devais les charmes et la
> beauté que vous me trouviez et dont vous me faisiez apercevoir]. [P. 68]

To break with this imaginary economy is to clear the way for
another, one in which her woman's worth cannot be calculated
in the terms of another's inflated discourse. Canceling the debt,
Mariana concludes that the *chevalier*, after all, took very little risk
within the closure of the limited society which is the convent.

As with the third letter, Mariana brings the final one to a close
by doubling back on her position so as to find another, more
significant, place from which to speak.

> I am mad to keep repeating the same things, I must leave you and
> not think of you anymore. I believe that I will not even write to you
> again. Am I obliged to give you an exact account of all my different
> feelings [suis-je obligée de vous rendre un compte exact de tous mes
> divers mouvements]? [P. 69]

The question is rhetorical but still poses an interpretive choice
for readers who would put something in the blank that follows it.
One could imagine, for example, Dora flinging similar words at
Freud as she left his office for the last time. And, on the evidence
of those final words on the page, the "case" of Mariana, like
Dora's case, might be judged a failure.

How do we write the end of *The Portuguese Letters?* In other words, what do we start writing at the point where Mariana stops? What would it mean to write, for example, that "there is no other way out except to stop writing. . . . Mariana's final decision, to stop writing, is truly the only authentic one. . . . Her repression is thus total?"[25] Why, in the case of Mariana, could one appear to be making sense with a notion such as "authentic repression?" We can only conclude that to read these letters toward such an end is to attempt the obliteration of Mariana's passage out of silence. But an ineradicable and immeasurable interval differentiates the silence which precedes this text from the blank that follows it. And in that blank, we are free to imagine a postscript not unlike the next letter Mariana proposed to write, a letter attesting to the success of her cure: "I want to write you another letter so as to show you that I will be more at peace perhaps in a little while . . . and that I only remember you when I want to do so!" (p. 68).

3 / A MOTHER'S WILL
The Princess de Clèves

> I am convinced that the dismantling of a single "phantom" can go
> as far as to modify the structure of the great abominable Truth—
> postulated but inexistent—which, nevertheless, rules the Uni-
> verse. Each time this happens, there is a small victory of Love over
> Death. Such is also the inspiration of the present essay.
> Nicolas Abraham, "The Interlude of 'Truth' "

 IT has become a commonplace to invoke *The Princess de Clèves* as France's first novel in the current sense and to credit its author, Madame de Lafayette, with the introduction of a number of techniques which were to guarantee the success of the genre. As with most *idées reçues*, this one has more place in a collective mythology than in literary history, since that history demonstrates the novel's gradual evolution rather than its sudden apotheosis.[1] Nonetheless, one is tempted to admit that as a mythical (rather than historical) origin, Mme de Lafayette's novel has a reasonable claim. Its setting is plausible yet unhampered by historical accuracy, thus distinguishing it from both the idyllic lack of context of the *grands romans* and the preemptive detail of the historical *mémoire*. Historical event intervenes more as a loosely structuring element, marking narrative time at intervals sufficient to signify duration. Peripheral characters appear only in their manifest roles as members of Henri II's court, while the central characters—Mme de Chartres, the prince and the princess, Nemours, and, to a lesser extent, the Vidame—are each represented at the juncture of their courtly exteriors with what is hidden, denied, or silenced by that appearance.

This last element of the novel constitutes no doubt its most important innovation of fictional technique, for it requires the intervention of a narrator who has no logical way of knowing what lies behind the various masks.[2] The impersonal, third-person narration simply bypasses the logic which had led to the other, more clumsy, narrative solutions of the period: the epistolary first-person or the indirect discourse of the *confident*. Mme de Lafayette's narrator presents no credentials underwriting the validity of what is told about that which, by definition, is meant to be hidden. Instead, the text takes the reader without transition from a prologue in which the dominant mode is historical anecdote to a series of fictional episodes where observable "event" is narrated over against a frequently contradictory analysis of that event by a character in the form of what Jean Fabre has called the interior narration. The obfuscation of the origin of this knowledge, instead of arousing the reader's suspicion, casts the narration in the incontrovertible form of an omniscient given, that which, in other words, is itself the origin of other, contingent modes of knowing. Thus, what the novel's characters may know or learn about themselves or each other is not so much discovered and recorded by the narrating agency as it is already generated by this all-knowing source which comprehends their necessarily limited knowledge.

The Princess de Clèves, then, to the extent that it figures an origin for a major mode of fictional narration, can do so precisely because it derives its psychological realism from the mythic principle of an original omniscience. On the other hand, the novel's force—both as a model for subsequent fiction and as a singular text—cannot be attributed to the confident representations of the narrator. On the contrary, it is the insistent recurrence of an enigma where none should be that, surreptitiously and without seeming to challenge the principle of a comprehensive knowing, takes hold of the reading we can give this text. Fabre, for example, admits to this effect at the end of his careful reading of the novel's analytic technique, the technique, that is, of the knowing narrator: "So much clairvoyance and one still ends up being an enigma for oneself as well as others."[3] Paradox is clearly one figure which lends familiarity to such a conclusion, or perhaps the critic had in mind the Pascalian formula for the explanation of the unexplainable: "The heart has reasons that reason ignores." Both of these figures, however, direct our attention away from the more puzzling relation between a comprehensive narration and an enigma.

The question is, then, one of a fictional construction which cannot wholly contain what is constructed. The excess is that strangeness or enigma which, as we've already suggested, sustains the interest or the force of the fiction. While one might consider all fiction in similar terms, Mme de Lafayette's novel dramatizes this dynamic in the relation it establishes between characters, specifically between a mother's construction and a daughter's excess.

Mme de Chartres's construction is her daughter, the young woman whose appearance at court signals the end of the historical introduction and the beginning of the fictional narrative: "There then appeared a beauty at Court who attracted everyone's gaze."[4] With the arrival of the girl and her mother, the calling of the roll of the courtiers and the mapping of the political lines of force at court are interrupted, taken over by fictional event, since among the host of named participants in the novel's affairs, Mme and Mlle de Chartres are the first totally invented characters. So as to make a place for this fiction within the pages of a recorded past, the future Princess de Clèves will be given a history, one which, naturally, traces her identity back to its parental source. It is thus as legitimate heiress rather than as unrecorded conception that Mlle de Chartres enters the network of alliances, her place in that network already inscribed:

> She was from the same family as the Vidame de Chartres and one of the richest heiresses in France. Her father had died young and left her in the care of Mme de Chartres, his wife, whose wealth, virtue and reputation were considerable. After losing her husband, she had spent several years away from the court. During this absence, she had devoted herself to the education of her daughter. [Pp. 247–48]

Unlike many of her fictional successors—for example, Rousseau's Julie or Laclos's Cécile—Mlle de Chartres is educated entirely in the bosom of her family, which is to say, by her mother. That instruction nonetheless derives its force and effectiveness from the erotic context which the later novelists make explicit by replacing the teacher/parent with a teacher/seducer, a

Saint-Preux or a Valmont.[5] In *The Princess de Clèves*, however, the scene of the girl's education effectively blocks this other scene of seduction rather than providing a pretext. The description of Mme de Chartres's education of her daughter thus represents a structure which will remain, in an important sense, unchanged throughout the novel. Yet what preserves this instruction from any shift in the direction of its erotic possibility is not, as one might suppose, an exclusion of that possibility but rather a far more effective form of its inclusion.

> [Mme de Chartres] did not endeavor only to cultivate her mind and her beauty. She also thought to instill virtue in her daughter and make it attractive to her. Most mothers imagine that it suffices never to speak of love's intrigue [*la galanterie*] in the presence of young women in order to divert them from it. Mme de Chartres held the opposite opinion. She often portrayed for her daughter scenes of love; she showed her its agreeable side so as to persuade her more easily to look at its dangerous side. She told her [*elle lui contait*] about men's falsity, their deceptions and their faithlessness, as well as the domestic unhappiness caused by love affairs. She made her see, on the other hand, the tranquillity of the faithful woman whose beauty and noble birth are enhanced by virtue. She also impressed upon her, however, how difficult it was to maintain this virtue without an extreme mistrust of oneself and without taking care to follow the only path that can lead to a woman's happiness: loving her husband and being loved by him. [P. 248]

This education is carried out not only during an absence from court but also in the absence of the father, whose death was the occasion for the withdrawal of mother and daughter from society. Yet the absence—of father, husband, society at large—also has a place within the couple as constituted. This is the most distinctive feature of Mme de Chartres's pedagogical method: "Most mothers imagine that it suffices never to speak of love's intrigue in the presence of young women in order to divert them from it. Mme de Chartres held the opposite opinion." Representing "love's intrigue," the mother's education comprehends it, assigns it a place in a narrative context. Sexual pleasure ("she showed her [love's] agreeable side") is thus not simply disallowed by the context of the mother's instruction but reinscribed as "dangerous." The appeal of the "agreeable," which has the force to undermine the lessons of virtue, is preemptively rechanneled so as, instead, to force the persuasiveness of the demonstration—"so as to persuade her more easily to look at its dangerous side." At the same time, the child is given to feel desire for a beyond-the-mother, that which is missing in their isolation from the world, and induced to locate the appeal of that absence in the mother's discourse.

This double moment—in which an outside appears and is at once reclaimed by the worldly-wise older woman, in which a sexual force is activated and at once harnessed—sets up the context for the narrative to follow: "She *told* her about men's falsity, their deceptions and their faithlessness, as well as the domestic unhappiness caused by love affairs." The absence of men from this initiation scene is negated inasmuch as the mother represents—both transitively and intransitively—an object for her daughter's desire, which is already to be found within the closed feminine couple. What is constructed by this mother's discourse functions both as denegation of that absence and as compensation for it. Thus, when Mme de Chartres hands over the key to happiness—"loving her husband and being loved by him"—it is a key which locks the door to the outside. The man who would enter this space of an introverted desire can do so only in a familiar guise, for the tranquillity which Mme de Chartres represents to her daughter will have become inseparable from the maternal presence (denegation of absence) to which it returns as to a source.

It is in these terms, then, that Mme de Chartres's narration of the world into which she will insert her daughter gives her a position comparable to that of the omniscient narrator. Like the narrator, whose story passes unproblematically between the manifest and the concealed levels of significance of an event, Mme de Chartres transgresses the limits which oppose her own discourse of virtue to that of its absent other, intrigue.[6] The enigma of Mlle de Chartres's desire, which is first articulated the day after her arrival at court, will take shape over against this construction.

> The day after her arrival, she went to match some precious stones at the house of an Italian who did a worldwide traffic in such things. . . . While she was there, the Prince de Clèves arrived. He was so taken aback by her beauty that he could not hide his sur-

prise. . . . M. de Clèves gazed at her in admiration and he could not imagine who this beautiful lady was whom he did not know. He understood by her manner and her attendants that she was of the highest rank. Because of her youth, he thought she was probably unmarried. As she was not accompanied by her mother, however, and as the Italian, who did not know her, addressed her as Madame, he did not know what to think and continued to look at her with amazement. . . . When she left, he consoled himself with the hope of learning who she was but he was surprised to discover that no one knew her. [Pp. 248–49]

Mlle de Chartres's appearance in the world poses a question which, until it can be answered, has an enigmatic power: who is "this beautiful lady whom nobody knows"? M. de Clèves takes the question to a general gathering of the court, where he receives, if not an answer, at least a reassurance that the strangeness he had encountered has no substance: "Madame said to him that there was no such person as the one he described, for if there were, everyone would know her" (p. 250). In effect, the following day, Mlle de Chartres is formally presented to the court and everything falls back into place for Clèves, "[who] was overjoyed to learn that this lady, whom he had found so lovely, was as well-born as she was beautiful" (p. 250).

Yet there is another level at which the enigma persists, another question posed by the appearance of the heroine in that jewelry shop. What is it that she has come looking for alone? What are these jewels that she covets for herself? Seeking to find a match for certain jewels or stones that she already possesses, the young woman has left her mother's house and come into the domain of a stranger, an Italian. It is there that the enigma is posed: the question is not the one that Clèves asks, "Who is this woman?"—the question of identity—but rather, "What does this woman want that she does not already have?" The precious stones that she brings with her, that part of her inheritance that she carries out of the maternal home, is brought to the stranger so that he might supply their mate, the jewel missing from the set her mother gave her. The missing piece of the puzzle is not Mlle de Chartres's name, the value of the stones already in her possession, but the name of another, in its hard brilliance, its perfect shape, and its inestimable worth.

Thus, the motive for Mlle de Chartres's visit to the jeweler's repeats and displaces the motive for her mother's return to court, a return which is prompted by the desire to find a match of equal value for the young woman. "Mme de Chartres, who was very proud, found that almost no one was worthy of her daughter. Thus, when she was in her sixteenth year, her mother brought her to court" (p. 248). That we might judge the value of Mme de Chartres's prize possession, there follows a brief physical description of the girl in which the word *éclat* suggests the brilliance of this family jewel: "Her fair skin and blond hair gave her a brilliance [*éclat*] such as no one had ever seen before. Her features were all regular and her general aspect and manner were full of grace and charm." It is, moreover, to a treasury of other families' jewels that Mme de Chartres brings her daughter in search of a mate. The introductory pages of the novel, in which the prominent members of the court are set before us one by one, serve as an inventory wherein the narrator, like the proprietor of a fine shop, lays out all the finest gems of the collection: "Never has a court gathered together so many lovely women and admirably handsome men. It seemed as if Nature had taken pleasure in endowing the greatest princesses and princes with her most beautiful gifts" (p. 242). The catalogue reserves special praise for the men on its list—"but what made this court particularly beautiful and magnificent was the infinite number of princes and great lords of special merit"—and characterizes those it will name as "the *ornament* and envy of their age." From among this rich display of nature's ornaments in human form, one stands out as "a masterpiece of nature": the Duke de Nemours, "the handsomest man in the world." He is the precious stone at the center of a display of magnificence and gallantry "which has never shown itself in France with such brilliance [*éclat*]" (p. 241). By virtue of his "incomparable valor and nobility," there was no lady at court who would not have been proud to pin him to her breast—"whose pride would not have been flattered to see him attached to her" (p. 244).

Among this assortment of crown jewels, Mlle de Chartres is put on display, "a perfect beauty [who] was envied and admired in a place where everyone was so accustomed to seeing beautiful ladies" (p. 247). To determine this new beauty's value, negotiations are begun whose success will depend on Mme de Chartres's complete knowledge of her daughter's position: "She urged her, not as her mother but as a friend, to confide in her all the gallant remarks addressed to her, and she promised to help her to find her way in these matters which were so often confusing for young people" (p. 253). This arrangement is simply an alternative form of the principle which guided the girl's education, that by which gallantry is both evoked as an outside and brought back home to mother. By its operation, the girl's intercourse with others is reenacted at home, with the mother as interlocutor, so that its danger can be assessed and avoided. And it is by means of just such an operation that the Prince de Clèves is chosen as the suitable husband, a match.

When Clèves first speaks to Mlle de Chartres of his passion and of his wish to marry her, he urges her to respond outside the limits imposed by the mother: "He urged her to make known to him her feelings for him and told her that those he felt for her were of a sort to make him eternally unhappy if she was only dutifully obeying her mother's will" (p. 257). Clearly, there is no such outside from which she can speak, no opening for a desire not already confined by her mother's instruction. The response she gives arises finally from this training and is empty of the content that Clèves has come seeking: "As Mlle de Chartres had a very noble, generous [*trés bien fait*: literally, well-made] heart, she was sincerely touched by the Prince de Clèves's conduct. Her gratitude imparted a certain sweetness to her responses and her words which sufficed to raise his hopes."

As a matter of course, Mlle de Chartres reports this conversation to her mother. Mme de Chartres praises the prince's conduct and tells her daughter that, if she wishes it, the marriage will be arranged. The daughter's answer to this proposal echoes the praise ("Mlle de Chartres answered that she had noticed the same good qualities in him") even as it remarks the absence of that particular element that would differentiate this echo from the mother's voice ("but that she felt no *particular* attraction for his person"). Thus, in this replay of the exchange between Clèves and his beloved, Mlle de Chartres answers the question put to her by her suitor: it is indeed duty rather than attraction that responds to Clèves. It is, in other words, to the mother, rather than the lover, that desire is spoken and then, necessarily, as absent from the exchange.

The marriage contract is concluded between Mme de Chartres and the prince on the following day. This detail underscores what the prince will later realize: that, to a significant degree, he is marrying the mother and not the daughter. Mme de Chartres, for her part, recognizes in the prince a man fit for the role she would have him play in her daughter's future. The mother's satisfaction with this arrangement may be read in the resolute ambiguity of the phrase "elle ne craignit point de donner à sa fille un mari qu'elle ne pût aimer en lui donnant le prince de Clèves" (p. 258). That is, "she did not fear that, by giving her daughter the Prince de Clèves, she was giving her a husband whom she could not love."[7] Is the fear she did not feel that her daughter would love her husband or that she would not? In either case, with these conditions written between the lines of the marriage contract, it is little wonder that the consummated union should satisfy the mother and leave the husband disappointed.

In effect, even before the celebration of the wedding, Clèves cannot mask his discontent. He complains to his future bride: "You feel only a certain kindness towards me which cannot satisfy me. You are neither impatient, nor worried, nor fretful." Mlle de Chartres protests: "I do not know what you want from me *beyond* what I am doing." The prince replies, taking up her image of a "beyond": "It is true . . . that you give me certain signs with which I would be content if there were something else *beyond*. . . . Neither your inclination nor your heart are touched by me and my presence neither pleases nor disturbs you." This exchange concludes when the narrator returns in order to confirm the prince's misgivings about the woman he loves. Mlle de Chartres, it would appear, simply does not understand. "Mlle de Chartres did not know how to answer. These distinctions were above her head. M. de Clèves saw only too well how far she was from the feelings which could satisfy him since it appeared to him that she did not even understand them" (pp. 258–59). In other words, the "beyond" which the prince desires is precisely that which lies beyond the knowledge imparted by a mother's education. Thus, although it is here, in dialogue with the lover, that the heroine is first represented in direct discourse, it is nonetheless still to the mother that she speaks.

For Clèves, marriage does not supply what is missing from their dialogue. As we have seen, that absence is already recuperated by the mother, with the result that what is consummated will inevitably be Mme de Chartres's "beyond" and not any other. This is made clear by the paragraph which follows the description of the wedding ceremony, the place in the text, in other words, that coincides with the consummation of that ceremony. The narrator, in effect, contrasts Clèves's dissatisfaction with Mme de Chartres's triumph, both of which are measured by the image of a "beyond."

> M. de Clèves did not find that Mlle de Chartres changed her feelings when she changed her name. The title of husband gave him greater privileges but no new place in his wife's heart. Thus, although now her husband, he did not cease to be her lover because he still had something to wish for *beyond* possession. Even though she lived perfectly well with him, he was not entirely happy. [P. 260]

On the other hand, jealousy has no part in the prince's sense of an incomplete possession of his new wife, for "no wife had ever been *further* from causing jealousy." This first suggestion of the distance which separates Mme de Clèves from the other wives at court is soon followed by another: "she had a manner which inspired such great respect and which appeared so far removed [*si éloignée*] from intrigue." The paragraph ends with a consolidation of these images of the princess's preeminent respectability which returns all credit to the *metteuse-en-scène*, the mother who has staged such a successful representation: "To her daughter's virtue, Mme de Chartres joined such a scrupulous observance of propriety that she managed to make her appear to be *a woman beyond anyone's reach* [*une personne où l'on ne pouvait atteindre*]" (p. 260). It is thus as the unattainable, untouchable woman that the Princess de Clèves graduates into the world without ever leaving the scene constructed by the mother.

It is at this point that the narrative picks up the adventures of the Duke de Nemours who, at last mention, had left the court to pursue his interests in England. The duke's departure is the last event of the introductory prologue, the final touch applied to the portrait of general court affairs as they stood at the moment of Mlle de Chartres's arrival. When the duke returns several months later, the position of the Princess de Clèves at court is firmly established. Nemours's reentry into the narrative is thus as a stranger into the familiar world of the heroine.

The princess is at a ball. As she is finishing a dance and "while she was looking around for someone she meant to take as her next partner," Nemours enters the hall in an unorthodox manner, climbing over chairs "to get to the dance floor" (p. 261). The king, wishing no doubt to be amused, shouts to her to take the man who has just arrived. It is then that the princess looks at this man.

> She turned and saw a man whom she thought at once could only be M. de Nemours. . . . This Prince was so handsome that it was difficult not to be surprised on seeing him for the first time. This was especially true when he had, as on this night, taken care with his appearance and was even more brilliant than usual. [Pp. 261–62]

The narrator reminds us, however, that "it was also difficult to see Mme de Clèves for the first time without amazement." The astonishment of this pair soon invades the entire assembly, for when they begin to dance together "a murmur of praise ran around the room." The murmur dissipates among the several voices in the crowd, each signaling an unnameability which has momentarily surfaced. The king and his entourage remark "something strange"; the Dauphine observes "something flattering"; the Chevalier de Guise notes "a certain embarrassment" on the princess's face and sums up the adventure as "something gallant and extraordinary." Finally, the princess's keenest observer, Mme de Chartres, cannot help but hear "a certain tone" in her daughter's account of the meeting.

The strangeness which surfaces and which sets off this charge of unnameable energy signals the difference between Mlle de Chartres's encounter with Clèves and Mme de Clèves's encounter with Nemours. Simply stated, in the first scene the heroine does not find what she has sought in the jewelry shop. In the second, "she was looking around for someone she meant to take" and is taken by surprise by Nemours. Mme de Clèves immediately recognizes the man coming toward her although she has never seen him before. She knows Nemours as strange, and their dance has the power to astonish the onlookers by this conjunction of the familiar and the unknown. "The King and the Queens remembered that they had never seen each other before and found that there was something strange in seeing them dance together without knowing each other." When the dance concludes, it is with the figure of "without knowing" that Mme de Clèves attempts to suppress the other, troubling, recognition, the moment in which she named Nemours to herself. Challenged by the Dauphine and by the duke himself to repeat this name out loud, to confess her secret knowledge the princess protests:

> "I assure you, Madame," answered Mme de Clèves, who seemed somewhat embarrassed, "I cannot guess as easily as you think."
>
> "You have guessed quite well," replied the Dauphine, "and there is even something flattering to M. de Nemours that you refuse to admit that you know him without ever seeing him before." [P. 262]

In other words, the first flattering mark the princess gives Nemours is this silent naming of a man she does not know. Once again, a distinction is drawn with the scene at the jeweler's, where an enigma is first posed about the princess's identity. As we saw, the question there cannot be answered by her name but only by the name of another. Here, the unknown person is supposed to be Nemours. As before, however, the question "Who is this person?" acts to disguise (although not to obscure) the princess's search for another "jewel" to match her own, a partner. In effect, the two scenes correspond in the mode of question and answer. It is henceforth with the secret name of Nemours that she will designate the desire that separates the mother's "unattainable woman" from this other self. Thus, the cleaving of the Princess de Clèves, first signaled by the split *parole* with which she names Nemours, will be measured by the transformation of the dialogue between mother and daughter.

As before, the daughter gives an account of her exchange with the man she has just met, but the mother remarks a difference: "she praised M. de Nemours to her with a certain tone that caused Mme de Chartres to conclude as had the Chevalier de Guise"; that is, that "she had been *touched* by the sight of this prince" (p. 263). What is touched, *atteint* from the outside, is precisely the closure of the mother—daughter dialogue, since, for the first time, an unspoken has arisen there, something which cannot be called by its name.

This deviation, however, cannot be wholly ascribed to a gap only in the daughter's speech: instead, the next narrative sequence, which is the first of the so-called digressions, comes along to fill a gap in the mother's discourse and to supply a crucial part of the maternal instruction which has been left unsaid. The story of Diane de Poitiers and Henri II, which is the story of a woman's duplicity and a man's unchanging devotion, could not have been told earlier without casting some doubt on the coherence of the representation of "men's falsity" that framed Mlle de Chartres's initiation into the world. Now, however, Mme de Clèves risks another danger if she is left in the dark any longer about her own capacity for duplicity and Mme de Chartres sees that the time has come to spell out the principle governing the social intercourse in which her daughter must engage. To the princess's complaint, "You have not informed me of the various interests and liaisons of the court," Mme de Chartres replies with the story of the court's central liaison, that between the king and his mistress, and prefaces the tale with its moral: "If you judge by appearance in this place . . . you will be often mistaken. Things are almost never what they seem" (pp. 264–65). The story thus serves not only to disabuse the princess of her own naive apprehension of courtly reality, but also to demonstrate that even a mother's word cannot always be trusted.

It is in the space of this new distrust beween mother and daughter that the princess gradually acknowledges her *inclination* for Nemours. At the same time, it is precisely through the silence that Mme de Chartres reads her daughter's desire. The narrator leaves no doubt about this articulation:

> [Mme de Clèves] found that she was less disposed to tell her mother what she thought of the Duke's attentions than she had been to speak to her about her other suitors. Without having decided to hide from her, she simply did not speak to her about this. But Mme de Chartres saw it only too well, along with the inclination that her daughter felt for him. *This knowledge was a painful one.*" [P. 270]

The mother's pain is inflicted by the thought of the daughter's peril ("she clearly saw the young woman's dangerous situation: loved by a man such as Nemours to whom she was also attracted") but it is conditioned by an exclusion of the mother from the daughter's speech. In other words, the painful knowledge Mme de Chartres gleans is not only the knowledge of the princess's *penchant* but also that it is no longer to her that the heroine is speaking truthfully.

This is the lesson to be learned from the complex of messages which are passed through the medium of the Maréchal de Saint-André's ball. Whereas Mme de Clèves issues one excuse (illness) to society at large for her absence from this important affair, she tells her mother that the real reason is her wish to discourage Saint-André in what she suspects are his hopes to impress her and win her affection. Mme de Chartres goes along with the masquerade even though she finds her daughter's explanation "peculiar." The day after the ball, however, Mme de Chartres discovers how her daughter had contrived to send an encouraging message to Nemours through this absence. As before, it is the Dauphine who serves as the princess's messenger when, in the presence of Nemours, Mme de Clèves, and Mme de Chartres, she supplies the link in their conversation. However, it is not only Nemours but also Mme de Chartres who gets the message, and her response is to detour the daughter's truth back into the closure of the mother's discourse. "At that moment, Mme de Chartres understood why her daughter had refused to go to the ball. Thus, in order to prevent M. de Nemours from reaching the same conclusion, she spoke up in a manner that seemed utterly sincere. 'I assure you, Madame . . . that she was truly ill' " (p. 274). Mme de Chartres's authority prevails for the moment: the Dauphine believes her; Nemours "was annoyed that this explanation sounded plausible"; and even Mme de Clèves, who had been embarrassed by the transparency of her own duplicity, "felt a certain regret" that her mother was able to lie more effectively and thereby efface the desired effect of the daughter's deceit. Having blocked the message to Nemours, Mme de Chartres becomes once again the sole possessor of the princess's truth.

It is important to note that, in this capacity, Mme de Chartres effectively displaces not only Nemours but also the Prince de Clèves. From the moment of the *coup de foudre* at the ball until the illness and death of Mme de Chartres, the prince is utterly absent as an actor in any of the narrated events and virtually disappears even as a point of reference in the narration of the princess's interiority. Thus, the conflict which produces that interiority first arises out of an opposition between Nemours and Mme de Chartres, lover and mother. It is only with a significant delay that the heroine acknowledges to herself that her desire for Nemours exists in relation to the absence of desire for Clèves. "Then she understood that the feeling she had for him was the one M. de Clèves had tried so hard to solicit from her. She found it shameful that she felt this way toward anyone but the husband who deserved her love" (p. 275). However, even this realization can have only a limited effect, for it too is produced in the context of the opposition between mother and lover, with the effect that when the husband is momentarily recalled from oblivion it is already as a representative of the mother's pole in that other, more fundamental, opposition. His significance for the princess is thus, as it has been from the outset, circumscribed by the mother's discourse.

Mme de Chartres's power to represent reality no longer derives from the absence which defined her daughter's education away from court. With the revelations of the story of Diane de Poitiers, the mother's discourse adopts a new strategy to maintain its representative value. Since "things are almost never what they seem," it is as an interpretive, rather than a descriptive, link to this deceptive world that Mme de Chartres continues to represent the truth of social exchange, even in the face of apparent contradiction. In the opposition with Nemours, therefore, Mme de Chartres has an almost unlimited advantage which she is careful to exploit. By interpreting certain appearances as deceptive, Mme de Chartres can insinuate that Nemours's apparent pleasure in the princess's company is merely a foil for "his great passion for the Dauphine." Mme de Clèves, in other words, risks becoming a screen for an illicit affair. This insinuation effectively displaces for a moment the reality of the other pattern which we have seen developing, the pattern of the Dauphine's function as mediator between the lovers. In that moment, however, Mme de

Clèves formulates what has, until then, remained "*sans dessein formé,*" unformulated. "What bitter pain she felt upon learning, through what her mother had just said to her, the interest she had taken in M. de Nemours. She had not yet dared admit it to herself" (p. 275).

Thus, to the mother's pain inflicted by the knowledge of her daughter's desire corresponds the daughter's pain in the knowledge of her own desire. In each moment, moreover, a danger is posited which operates as a screen for that other danger which is the developing gulf between mother and daughter. For Mme de Clèves, as we have seen, the image of her husband briefly surfaces on the other side of this gulf but fades again when she reflects on the mother's representation: "She felt hurt and embarrassed by the fear that M. de Nemours had only sought to use her as a pretext for his affair with the Dauphine. *This thought decided her* to tell Mme de Chartres what she had not yet told her." In effect, it is the mother's misrepresentation of her daughter's sexual position that conditions the princess's first thoughts of renouncing that position so as to return to the safe harbor of a mother's all-encompassing understanding. The princess determines that, given the fraudulence of the dialogue with Nemours, her truth still resides in the connection to the mother.

The narrative sequence which is organized around the event of Mme de Chartres's death is introduced by the deferral of this resolution to speak: "She went the next morning into her room to execute her resolution. She found, however, that Mme de Chartres had a slight fever so that she did not want to speak to her" (p. 275).[8] Instead of speaking to her mother, Mme de Clèves talks to the Dauphine, who persuades her that Nemours's evident lovesickness cannot be diagnosed as Mme de Chartres has suggested. Having dismantled her mother's misrepresentation, the princess "found that, in spite of herself, she was in a calmer and happier mood than she had been earlier" (p. 276). This pleasant interlude ends, however, with the heroine's return to her mother's side, where she discovers that, while she had been entertaining gratifying thoughts of her lover, Mme de Chartres's fever had risen dangerously high.

It is no longer a question for Mme de Clèves of confessing, as she had resolved to do. The pain of separation, which before was represented by a daughter's silence, is now overtaken by "an extreme anxiety" in the face of the ultimate separation which is the mother's imminent death, the gulf which no mere words can bridge. Necessarily also, therefore, Nemours's presence at this scene functions as a relief from her anxiety—"she could not keep herself . . . from being pleased at the sight of him"—but in his absence ("when she did not see him") Mme de Clèves rediscovers a pain which she identifies as follows: "She thought that the charm she found in his company was the beginning of passion and she almost believed she hated him for the pain that this thought gave her" (p. 277). The presence and absence of the lover is thereby coordinated with pleasure and pain but that pain is reassimilated back into the terms of her separation from the mother, that "beginning of passion" that has placed distance between her and Mme de Chartres.

Through Mme de Chartres's parting speech, this pain will take on its definitive association: it is the child's pain not at the thought of losing the mother but at the thought that that loss is what the child desires. Mme de Chartres speaks to her daughter for the last time from her deathbed and what she says confirms that the gulf of silence between them has had a reality only for the child: "You are attracted to M. de Nemours. I do not ask you to confess it to me. . . . For a long time now I have been aware of this attraction." Thus, instead of a confession scene by means of which the child crosses back over into the mother's comprehensive embrace, another scene is being enacted wherein the confession is already too late, *de trop*, and ineffective in its aim to bridge a gap. The bridge of the mother's unfailing knowledge has always been there; if the child has not seen it, it is because she has desired to look in another direction, and to keep silent. The metaphor with which Mme de Chartres represents her daughter's position is chosen to this effect: "You are on the edge of the precipice. It will take a great, violent effort to hold yourself back" (pp. 277–78). Once in place, the image of the precipice continues to organize Mme de Chartres's rhetoric as she exhorts her daughter to choose "duty" and "virtue" and to flee the dangers of "gallantry." As the speech draws to a close, however, Mme de Chartres evokes her impending death: "If anything could spoil the happiness I hope for in leaving this world, it would be to see you fall like other women; but if this misfortune must overcome you, then I face death joyfully for at least I will not be witness to such a thing" (p. 278). The dangerous precipice is reinvoked here, but through the context it has acquired a supplementary meaning. The mother, as well, is balanced at the edge of an abyss, that of her own death. Mme de Chartres's final message derives its force through this shift from the daughter's peril to the mother's fate; only the daughter's virtue, her flight from the chasm that is open before her, can preserve the mother from her own descent into misfortune and destruction. The princess, in other words, can choose to keep her mother alive.

Keeping the mother alive will take the form, primarily, of designating a substitute. In the wake of Mme de Chartres's death, therefore, the Prince de Clèves, who has been waiting in the wings, will move into the role vacated by his mother-in-law. The substitution occurs as Mme de Clèves is overtaken by grief at her loss—grief in which "the need she felt for her mother, to defend her against M. de Nemours, continued to have [a major part]." For the first time since her engagement, the princess is presented in dialogue with Clèves: "She was friendlier and more loving with him than she had ever been. She was unhappy when he left her for it seemed that, if she clung to him, he would defend her against M. de Nemours" (p. 278). It is thus in the mode of the mother's designated representative in the opposition to Nemours that Clèves takes his wife away from court.

The first interlude in the country is represented almost entirely by the break in the central narrative which is the digression concerning Mme de Tournon. It is also through his position as narrator of this story that Clèves fully assumes the mother's place in relation to the heroine. That position is mapped at several junctures. First, the distance which isolates the princess from the world of the court is bridged by the person of Clèves and, even more importantly, by the representation of the affairs of that world which he brings with him when he joins her in her retreat. In this manner, that retreat reproduces the conditions of her education during the absence of her mother from court. Second, the story he tells of Mme de Tournon's duplicity disabuses Mme de Clèves of her own naive assumption of the lady's virtue; its effect is such that Clèves could well have prefaced his story, as

Mme de Chartres had done, with the caution that "things are almost never what they seem." Like the story of Diane de Poitiers, then, the tale of Mme de Tournon serves to set the princess on guard against her own duplicity within the context of a false belief in her woman's virtue. "You praise me more than I am worth" (p. 280) replies Mme de Clèves to her husband's ready assumption that she, unlike Mme de Tournon, has nothing to hide. Clèves, however, continues with his story.

While these conjunctions with the mother's pedagogical/ representational role function through structural repetitions in the narrative, a third conjunction is put in place when Clèves explicitly claims for himself the mother's prerogative to receive a daughter's confession. This conjunction is noted by the narrator and provides the connection which integrates this peripheral narrative into the central one. It occurs when Clèves insists that the advice he has given his friend is the same he himself would follow:

> "I am giving you the same advice that I would follow myself," I said to him. "I value sincerity so highly that I believe if my mistress, or even my wife, confessed to me a weakness for someone else, I would be distressed but not embittered. *I would give up the role of lover or husband in order to advise and console her.*" [P. 284]

The narrator intervenes at this point for the first time since Clèves began his story in order to register Mme de Clèves's silent reception of this lesson: "These words made Mme de Clèves blush for she saw their relation to her own situation. This surprised and upset her. It was a long moment before she recovered her composure." Clèves, in this moment, offers his wife what she has implicitly sought from him: that he relinquish the position of husband/lover for that of adviser/mother. The promise to do so, however, is troubling and the invitation to speak is finally ignored, at least for now.

It is at this point, then, that the enigma of the Princess de Clèves reemerges, in a mode which recalls its earlier manifestation in the jewelry shop. Why does Mme de Clèves respond with only silence to her husband's invitation to speak? Why does she hesitate to resume the dialogue with the mother at the precise point where it was interrupted, that is, at the moment of her confession, which Clèves here designates hypothetically—"if my mistress, or even my wife, confessed to me a weakness for someone else." If, as we have suggested, the princess chooses to keep the mother alive, why refuse this occasion to resuscitate her *parole*? Is there not, as in the jewelry shop, something left out of the mother's will, something, indeed, which she also chooses to keep alive in this moment of silence? The enigma as it was first posed—what does she want?—has thus been reformulated: who—or what—does the princess want to keep alive?—which is also to ask, who—or what—must die?

The importance of this question, we find, has been displaced onto an episode from the margins of the central intrigue, that part of the narration which serves as historical frame for the fiction. It is an episode which itself poses an enigma and which places the issue of "who must die" at the very center of the court's attention, since the death in question is that of the king.

The court, having idly debated the reliability of astrological prediction, is divided in its opinion when the king takes his turn to speak. His intervention, in effect, closes off the debate, but not before the riddle of a king's death is put in place.

> A few years ago, an astrologer of considerable reputation visited the Court. Everyone went to see him, including myself, but I did so without telling him who I was. I took MM. de Guise and d'Escars with me and I made them go before me. The astrologer, however, addressed me first, as if he judged me to be the others' superior. Perhaps he knew who I was. In any case, he told me something which would have been quite inappropriate if he knew me. He predicted that I would be killed in a duel. . . . Finally, we all left very disappointed with the astrologer. I do not know what will happen to MM. de Guise and d'Escars, but it is very unlikely that I will be killed in a duel. The King of Spain and I have just signed a peace treaty. Even if we had not done so, I doubt that we would fight each other and that I would challenge him to a duel as my father challenged Charles V. [Pp. 296–97]

The astrologer's prediction is puzzling because its form recognizes the king's preeminence while its message denies it. Henri therefore hesitates between the belief that the astrologer knew he was speaking to the king and the belief that he did not. The courtiers, however, are unanimous in adopting the second hypothesis, which closes the debate. The court, in this moment, realizes its function as a political unit stabilized through identification with the king by retreating before the enigma of the king's identity.

Henri, of course, dies as predicted, the victim of Montgomery's lance in a festival tournament. As he watches his king being carried from the stadium, the Constable recalls the prophecy: "The Constable remembered, in that moment, the prediction that the King would be killed in singular combat. He had no doubt that this prediction had been accomplished" (p. 356). What has also been accomplished, however, is a solution to the enigma of the king's identity as it was posed by the question: Who will die? In effect, his death operates to distinguish the representation of sovereignty from the representative sovereign. In other words, Henri dies, but the king lives. It can now appear that the astrologer's prediction was obscured by the mortal representative's exercise of an immortal power.

As portrayed in *The Princess de Clèves*, the death of Henri II functions as more than an historical event whose inclusion in the narrative signals duration and imparts verisimilitude. In this novel, as in general, the death of a king is also symbolic, which is to say that it occurs not only along the temporal axis of succession but also according to the timeless principle of substitution. François II gains the throne, therefore, both as the son following the father and as the representative of sovereign power, as the symbol of the stable definition of the State. That stability, in other words, relies both on a differentiation of the son from the father (to allow for succession) and on a suppression of this difference (to preserve the power that is symbolized from historical accident).

The symbolic value of this particular moment of royal transition for the rest of the narrative is brought into play still further into the margins, at the point where the boundaries of this text begin to dissolve into an intertextual network. That point of contact is established, one might say, by the point at which Montgomery's lance makes contact with the body of the king: "He charged; their lances broke and a splinter from Montgomery's landed in the King's eye and lodged there" (p. 356). The king dies blinded and thus able at last to see how the prophecy of his fate has been realized. Through this ironic insight, Mme de Lafayette's historical monarch is placed in a line of descent from the mythical king of Thebes, Oedipus. This allusion serves to highlight that other vehicle of the comparison which has been in place since the prologue: Henri's liaison with Diane de Poitiers, the woman who was also his father's mistress and whose power displaces that of the legitimate queen.

There is perhaps a measure of political critique in the implicit parallel with a mythical king who reigned over the disintegration of his nation. Might Mme de Lafayette be pointing to an exercise of power which tips the precarious balance too far in the direction of an effacement of difference, a blurring of the distinction between the representative sovereign and the represented sovereignty? When Oedipus takes his mother as wife, he assumes his father's place within a structure which is defined by the exclusion of precisely that substitution, a structure, in other words, which maintains/is maintained by the differentiation of parent and child. The resulting confusion is not only within the generational order but also within the representational order: Oedipus's accession to the throne is not as the representative of the former sovereign. That is, his accession illustrates the paradox whereby patricide is at once the only means of acquiring the father's power and the means by which the legitimacy of that power is subverted; thus Oedipus, in the very act of killing the father, kills the only legitimate source of the sovereignty which he would have. It is only in his difference that the son can assume an exercise of power which will not be buried with his father. If there is political critique, therefore, it might carry an implicit warning that succession to the throne of Louis XIV is already menaced by just such a confusion of the present sovereign with the power he represents.

If, however, the Oedipal myth is evoked as we have described, then it brings with it more than a discreet reference to court politics. The myth may also serve as a key to the princess's enigma, a key which lies in the differentiation of parent and child, or, more exactly, of the parent's desire from that of the child. The question of "who must die" organizes the mythic elements around the only apparent answers: the child or the parent. Yet, it is because the prophecy of Oedipus's fate attributes to the child the desire *of* the parent (which is also desire *for* the parent) that the homicidal solution is invoked. Whence, then, comes the conviction in the prophecy's truth if not from the truth which is already in place, the fantasy of a child who will represent one's own desire? If so, it is not the child who must be executed but the wish that masks itself as a prophetic truth, the representation which screens a parent's desire behind that of the newly born. It is, in other words, the fantasized representation of the child, not the child, and, as well, the fantasy of the parent, not the parent, which must be put to death or, at least, must not be allowed to become the only representation of desire. Killing the parent's "child" thus becomes the process of elaborating these other representations, of assuming a position in relation to the desire of another who is "not-the-parent." Another force will have to be brought into play, a force which is not already circumscribed by the original given of a parent's construction.[9]

For the princess, this execution will be staged and restaged, for on each such occasion the original representation of "the unattainable woman" remains in force. In the scene of the famous confession, for example, the princess speaks both as a woman beyond reach and as a woman *atteinte*, that is, touched and tainted by passion. It is this double determination which Nemours, after a first moment of elation, understands: "He realized that the same thing which had just let him know he had touched Mme de Clèves's heart must also convince him that he would never receive any sign of this passion. It was impossible to compromise a woman who had resorted to such an extraordinary remedy" (p. 337). Finally, however, the scene of the confession fails in its execution because, by its very structure, it substitutes, for the representation of a mother's desire, the representative—the Prince de Clèves.

Mme de Clèves decision to speak to her husband is clearly inscribed in the conjunction noted between Mme de Chartres's discourse and that of the prince.

> She remembered everything that Mme de Chartres had told her before she died and the advice she had given to use any means, however difficult they might be, to avoid entering into an affair.

> What M. de Clèves had said about sincerity . . . also came back to
> her. It seemed to her that she ought to confess to him her attraction
> for M. de Nemours. [P. 303]

When Mme de Clèves finally acts on her resolution, it is, as she
later reflects, "almost without intending to do so" (p. 337). In
effect, her admission to Clèves, like the earlier aborted confession to her mother, is accomplished through the other's com-
prehension of silence. Pressed by her husband to explain her
withdrawal from court affairs, Mme de Clèves avows the reason
when she points to her inability to confess:

> "Do not constrain me," she said to him, "to confess to you a thing
> that *I do not have the force to confess* even though I have intended to
> do so several times. Let it be enough to say that prudence would
> advise a woman of my age, who is mistress of her own conduct, not
> to remain exposed at Court."
> "Whatever are you trying to suggest, Madame?" cried M. de
> Clèves. "I would not dare to say it for fear of offending you."
> Mme de Clèves did not answer and *her silence* was the final blow
> that confirmed what her husband was thinking.
> *"You do not answer me,"* he continued, "and *that tells me* that I am
> not mistaken." [P. 333]

The prince supplies the force of the confession, just as Mme de
Chartres had done when she announced to her daughter: "You
are attracted to M. de Nemours." In this mode, the dialogue with
Clèves resurrects the final dialogue with the mother.

At the same time, however, this scene is functioning to force a
wedge in the princess's *parole*, to distinguish it from that produced by the mother's construction. This distinction is indicated
by Nemours's unknown intrusion as another interlocutor.
Through his intervention, Mme de Clèves cannot speak only in
the mode of the already-understood, silent exchange with the
mother. The exchange is doubled by Nemours's position as the
destinataire of her avowal of desire, and Clèves cannot reappropriate this interruption back into a version of maternal com-
prehension. The word is out.

It is thus that Clèves remains ignorant of the answer to his
question "Who is he?" while on the other hand, Nemours, who
poses the question as well ("he could not forgive M. de Clèves for

giving up his effort to discover the name that his wife was hiding from him" [p. 335]), is alone able to read an answer in her confession of the fate of her portrait. To Clèves's insistence that she reveal the name, the princess replies: "It is useless to insist. . . . *I have the force to silence* what I believe should not be spoken." The force to close off the dialogue with the mother is the force which, from the beginning, has sustained the dialogue with the lover. In effect, the princess's refusal to name Nemours reproduces the moment at the ball in which the silencing of that name elicited the first mark of her "flattery."[10] Thus, the scene which is enacted here confronts two different forces, two modes of silence in the princess's speech: the first, which says, "I do not have the force to confess," is a silence whose force is supplied by the mother, as by "someone who could console her and give her strength [*de la force*]" (p. 279); the second, which says, "I have the force to silence," is the silence whose force is other and by means of which one reaches the outside of the closed fortress constructed by a mother's love.

The dialogue with the husband plots the juncture of these two forces. In speaking to Clèves, the princess is speaking both to the mother's representative and to another who cannot be completely assimilated by this substitution. It may be indeed at this level of ambiguous conjunction that the proper names of Mme de Lafayette's protagonists suggested themselves to her. *Chartres* would reside in the castrated (*châtré*) realm of no desire while the lover's name figures the negativity of passion—*ne-amour*. As for *Clèves*, if one hears the verb *cliver*, to split, to sever, then what of its other, intransitive, usage which survives in English: to cleave, that is, to adhere to, to cling, to be faithful to? The Prince de Clèves, in other words, is semantically situated at the junction of a cleavage, or *sevrage*, and its contrary, adhesion, just as he is placed between mother and lover.

The confession is structured not only by these forces but also by the geographical opposition which has been in place since the description of Mlle de Chartres's education: the court as the outside of the mother's construction, the locus of *galanterie,* and the country as that place where one is safe from *les hommes galants*. Mme de Chartres's cartography appropriately provides her last advice to her daughter: "Have strength [*de la force*] and courage, my child. Withdraw from the Court, oblige your husband to take you away" (p. 278). That the confession takes place in the country, at Coulommiers, places it in a series of other such moments of retreat—for example, the moment after the death of Mme de Chartres, when space is required in which to reconstruct the threatened edifice.

The return to court after the admission precipitates the dissolution, once again, of that construction. This is signaled by the disintegration of Clèves's position as maternal representative. His desire—marked by the acts of jealousy—is more clearly than ever *de trop*, that is, unassimilable to the space of nondesire constructed by the mother. His impulse to know what his wife conceals, to force her, in other words, to name her desire to him, is set to work eroding sincerity, the mode of exchange he shared with Mme de Chartres. Clèves's jealousy shatters the closed imaginary structure within which the princess has articulated her desire for an outside. It is thus in order to regain her place in that structure that Mme de Clèves again retreats to Coulommiers, this time alone.

At Coulommiers, behind barricades "which were very high. . . to prevent anyone from entering" (p. 366), stands a garden pavilion, a fantasylike construction whose layout has earlier been described in a detailed manner that contrasts sharply with the generally imprecise classical prose of the novel (p. 332). (The fascination exercised by the pavilion is also illustrated by Mme de Martigues, who, after returning from a visit to Coulommiers, responds to the queen's inquiry about Mme de Clèves with a description of the place: "Mme de Martigues, who had found Coulommiers delightful, told of all its beauties. She went into particular detail in her description of the forest pavilion" [p. 365].) Here, within the fragile glass walls of the structure, out of reach, unattainable, the solitary princess may safely go through the motions of a passionate encounter. Her activities—tying ribbons the color of her hair around a cane belonging to Nemours, staring with rapture at his portrait—function, as Michel Butor has observed, like elements of a dream, displacing sexual significance onto innocent objects and gestures.[11]

Outside this structure and excluded from the ritual stands

Nemours. Seeing himself represented at the center of the princess's dream, he desires to take up that place for himself. But first
he must pass the threshold of the fantasy construction. "Urged
on all the same by the desire to speak to her and reassured by
everything he had seen which raised his hopes, he advanced a
few steps, but he was trembling so much that a scarf he was
wearing got caught in the window so that he made a noise" (p.
367). Nemours's advance on the isolated woman is halted by the
construction that defines her imaginary closure. His impulse to
speak to Mme de Clèves and thus to transgress the limits of their
silent exchange is here translated by an inadvertent noise as the
window catches at his person. It is as if the structure itself must
crack to allow him to enter. Before it can give way, Mme de
Clèves, having been alerted by the noise, has retreated still
further inside, until she is once again out of reach.

Nemours's entanglement in the open doorway gives both participants in the scene room to speculate on what has happened.
Neither can be certain that the princess has recognized the man
at the window as Nemours. In this fashion, the incident at the
pavilion replays another circumstance of their first meeting at
the ball, when Nemours entered the familiar circle of the princess: "She was dancing with M. de Guise, there was a lot of noise
at the door to the room, as of someone entering and causing a
stir. . . . She turned and saw a man who she thought at once
could only be M. de Nemours, who was climbing over chairs to
get to the dance floor" (p. 261). As in the original moment, when
the first sign of desire lets itself be read in a negated recognition,
this scene ends with a similar deferral as the lovers are led to
suspend the "events" of the encounter from the tenuous thread
of their own desire. The suspension of certain knowledge sets up
the pattern for the missed encounters which proliferate in the
later section of the narrative—at the silk merchant's shop, in the
public garden, and finally, in the most explicit repetition of the
scene at the pavilion, across the courtyard, when the lovers
furtively catch sight of one another: "In the morning, she first
went to see if there might be someone at the window which
looked out on her house. She went and there she saw M. de
Nemours. This surprised her and she withdrew so quickly that
the Prince realized he had been recognized" (p. 381).

The coy speculation of the lovers, which allows them to sustain the enigmatic space of the erotic encounter, has its counterpoint in the account of the extrinsic observer. The spy whom Clèves has sent on the heels of Nemours is careful to qualify this account as a limited one when he reports to his master: "I have nothing to tell you . . . with which to make a certain judgment. It is true that M. de Nemours entered the garden in the forest two nights in a row" (p. 372). The speculative space which the faithful servant leaves open for his master—the space beyond the garden wall—is one which Clèves will not enter, choosing instead to cut short the trail of the enigma and cast the uncertain events in the garden in an unequivocal light: " 'That is enough,' replied M. de Clèves, giving him the sign to withdraw, 'that is enough and I do not need any more enlightenment.' " Cutting short the enigma, Clèves seals off the space of desire with a certain knowledge that it is he who must die.

Just as the Prince de Clèves functioned as a living substitute for the dead mother, his death is also prescribed by this structure of repetition.[12] Indeed, that death, which is precipitated by the signs of his wife's infidelity, makes explicit what has to remain hidden in the causal chain that produces the death of the mother. That is, the fatal consequences of her betrayal of Clèves serve in part to reimplicate her in the circumstances of Mme de Chartres's death: her unavowable, undeniable crime is still that of the daughter's infidelity to the mother's fantasy of impervious womanhood. At the same time, however, as Clèves's death reproduces that of the mother, it also comes as a fatal effect of just such a failure to differentiate mother and husband. His death, in other words, can be retraced to the very structure with which the princess attempts to guard against another demise, that of the passionless woman. "She" must not be allowed to die even if her "life" must be bought at the price of another's, at the price, finally, of one's "own."

With the death of Clèves, this construction is once again menaced with extinction. "What dormant passion was rekindled in her heart and with what violence! [Nemours] appeared to her as . . . [a man] to whom she was so strongly attracted that she would have loved him even if he did not love her. . . . No longer did duty or virtue oppose her feelings. All the obstacles were lifted" (p. 380). The revival of desire for the lover, however, brings with it a renewal of the painful guilt of separation, and the heroine's thoughts soon turn to her crime: "She gave in to these thoughts which were so *opposed to her happiness* . . . [and] she returned home, convinced that she had to flee his presence as something entirely *opposed to her duty*" (pp. 380–81). As before, the heroine resolves to deny the intervention of death and thus of her own desire, which has placed her at the crumbling edge of a precipice. The opposition is therefore redrawn between the lover, happiness, and the danger of a fall, on the one side, and the mother (husband), duty, and the safety of flight from the gaping hole on the other.

The final interview with Nemours is conducted across this gulf. One can only imagine his dismay when, after successfully maneuvering the princess into a *tête-à-tête*, Nemours discovers that, after all, they are not alone—a ghost has risen up and taken form in his mistress's discourse: " 'Oh! Madame,' said M. de Nemours to her, 'what is this *ghost of duty* with which you oppose my happiness?' " (p. 387). Each time the spectre is held up before him, Nemours attempts to dispatch it with a contrary appeal. In her final words to him, the princess can only plead for time to put the ghost to rest: " 'It is true,' she replied, 'that I am sacrificing much to a duty that lives only in my imagination. Wait and see what time can do. M. de Clèves has only just died and this mournful fact [*cet objet funeste*] is so recent that it still clouds my view' " (p. 389).

It is, of course, a contrary effect which is already in place: keeping Clèves alive is the means of staying any movement along the axis of desire. "I must remain in my present situation and keep the promises I have made never to leave it for another" (p. 388). The danger to the memory of the other masks the danger to the self, or rather to the construction of the inviolate self. Giving a permanent home to *"cet objet funeste"* anchors this construction firmly in time before it can fall into the experience of a loss which would be its shattering demise: "The certainty that I have of one day losing your love seems to me such a horrible fate that, even if I did not have reasons of duty which are insurmountable, I doubt that I could ever decide to risk that fate. . . . It would cause me a mortal pain" (p. 387–88). Keeping the "other" alive, then, keeps safe the fiction of the invulnerable self.

The flight of the Princess de Clèves has its meaning in this refusal of a certain death—the death of a representation in which figures a mother's desire for the child-woman. Her retreat first to a country estate and finally to a convent functions in effect to make literal the figure of "the unattainable woman." Her withdrawal is also a return—a return to the mother who, as a young widow, left court for a more tranquil existence. It is thus inevitably another death which the princess must embrace in her escape from the mortal threat of desire. Upon reaching her country home, the heroine, "whose mind had been so troubled," falls gravely ill and hovers close to death. "This prolonged and intimate view of death made the things of this life appear in a different light to Mme de Clèves. The necessity of death, which she saw as very near, led her to feel detached from everything." Keeping the (m)other alive and thereby keeping intact the representation of the integral self have their complement in this submission to a premature death of "this life."

The death of the princess is recorded, in passing, by the final sentence of the novel: "Her life, which was rather short, left examples of inimitable virtue" (p. 395). Once again, a representation is saved from the fate of the representative, since the princess, as well, leaves a ghost as she departs the world: the insubstantial remains of an incomparable virtue. Her death, in other words, sustains and consolidates the construction of an unattainable, inimitable model. In its stead, the unmatched force of the heroine's desire, that cleft of difference which detaches the child from the mother, the reproduction from the model, expires without a trace. This effacement, thus, is but the final effect of the repeated failure to differentiate between Mother and her constructions, the failure, in other words, to bury the parent's remains. It is only in the space—the gap—uncovered by such a differentiation that the Princess de Clèves might, herself, have ceased to be just another product of a mother's fantasy.

4 / UNDERGROUND ROUSSEAU
Julie, or the New Heloise

I have always loved water passionately and the sight of it plunges
me into delightful daydreams which often have no clear direction.
The Confessions

 IN suggesting that Mme de Clèves's retreat into a
cloister reproduces her mother's withdrawal from
court on the death of her husband, I wish to signal
the overdetermination of the closure that ends Mme
de Lafayette's novel. Not only does the princess close off her
dialogue with Nemours, but she does so in a fashion that restores
the context of the mother's unique instruction. In this sense, she
returns to the single source of the identity of "unattainable
woman," the point from which it is once again possible to
imagine its truth and thus to give the dead mother what she
wants: the princess's example of "inimitable virtue." Ending as
it began, the narration describes a sterile circle of the heroine's
enclosure by the force of the mother's uninterrupted representation. This construction finally prescribes a deadly refusal of the
desired exchange with the absent other of the mother-daughter
identity.

In this chapter, I propose to open the locks on another fiction of
closure: that of an imagined paternal identity preserved by a
daughter's virtue. This shift to the patriarchal mode of the exclusion of woman's desire does not, however, simply restore the
missing term of Mlle de Chartres's initiation. Rather, a certain
maternity has been covered over here and follows below ground
the path to another source.

97

Julie, or the New Heloise: that title would seem to set out the terms of an analogy. Rousseau was, no doubt, appealing to the considerable number of his contemporaries who, for more than fifty years, had shown an insatiable appetite for the story of Heloise and an ever-increasing tolerance for new twists in the old tale. The year 1758—during which Rousseau was revising his novel—marks perhaps a summit in the Heloise fad, what the leading historian of the legend has described as "a delirious enthusiasm, an exuberant flowering, an overflowing of works on this already overworked subject."[1] Approaching the novel today in the Bibliothèque de la Pléiade's critical edition, we read that the suggested analogy of the title was a kind of afterthought which points only to a loose set of parallels thrown over the text in a superficial fashion.[2] Rousseau, suggest the editors, can be forgiven this lapse into passing fashion, but it would be a travesty to give the alternative title more than a passing remark.

As we will have occasion to see more clearly in what follows, editorial commentary on this novel can have the effect of diverting readers away from the text's most obvious devices, such as, for example, the title. In this instance, it is the other name in that title which can be disregarded without loss. In this, the editors may be cooperating with a general tendency of the novel's discourse to elide a woman's name or at least to replace it with other words, a tendency which we will analyze in this chapter. As I will suggest, this diverting of the reader's attention works, inadvertently perhaps, to locate a danger to the reader or indeed a danger in the reading process.

If, however, such a warning is concealed in the dismissal of the other name for the heroine in the title, how then does the modern editor's caution conjugate with that of the text's first "editor," Rousseau, as he phrases it in the preface: "No chaste girl has ever read novels. I have chosen a sufficiently decisive title for this one so that upon opening it one would know what the story was. She who, in spite of this title, would dare to read a single page is lost" (p. 6). I will return to this warning at an appropriately dangerous moment in the text of the novel, but I want here to consider the danger which is already signaled even before the novel begins—by its title.

The phrase "a sufficiently decisive title" poses a problem to the reader of this novel with more than one name: *Julie, or the New Heloise: Letters of Two Lovers, Inhabitants of a Small Town at the Foot of the Alps.* Is the title which Rousseau had in mind in his preface one or more of these several designations, considered separately or together? What is it in the title that tells the reader—"the chaste girl" in particular—what the story is? The subtitle—*Letters of Two Lovers, etc.*—is certainly more descriptive than the alternative titles, which are denominative. Of course, *The New Heloise* invokes more than just a proper name, since "Heloise" brings with it already, metonymically, the story of two lovers. Finally, we might ask, what is decisive or decided about a title which is presented in the form of an alternative?

Rousseau, nonetheless, took pains to assure that "the single or double title contains everything [he] put into it and yet that it not be confused."[3] He himself prefers the double solution: "I think that the title should be divided and that there should be two of them instead of just one. The first will have only the words 'Julie or the New Heloise. Part One.' The second will include the rest."[4] Here, the author, writing to his editor, is using the term "title" in the printer's sense of "title page" and thus is requesting two rather than one such pages, each to carry part of the full title. Rousseau is thus requesting an unusual disposition since the full title—"everything that he put into it"—will appear on no single page, whereas customarily, when two title pages are used, the first carries the title alone and is called the "false title (page)" while the second carries both title and subtitle and is called the "title (page)." In any case, the reader, in order to learn the full title of this novel, must turn a page. She must, in other words, already go beyond the title (the false title?) in order to read the rest, without which the several parts would become confused.

If doubling the title page is meant to prevent confusion, then it is precisely because it is double that the title can constitute such a clear warning to the girl's chastity. "She who, in spite of this title, would dare to read a single page is lost." That is, any girl who has already turned the page to read title and subtitle has also already begun to read doubly, to seek out the title beneath the title, one name beneath the other. This process is here, at the beginning, made to coincide with the act of reading one page after another. Since reading the title cannot be a simple act, the girl who does so is forewarned that by continuing to turn the pages she will be continuing within a duplicitous mode and one which, therefore, undermines her title to chastity, making of it but a "false title."[5]

Beyond the "dangerous" implications of the spacing of the complex title, another level of the text's significance may be lost if the name Heloise is dismissed as superficial to the structure of the work it announces. In effect, this assumption already takes for granted no more than a surface understanding of the figure of Heloise, one which, in other words, ignores that, like *Julie*, *Heloise* is a text to be read. Rather than signaling a reference to some static reality, Rousseau's double title defines an intertextual system.[6]

In the first part of this chapter, I will begin a double reading of this novel by recalling some of the analyses already outlined in the first chapter on the correspondence of Heloise and Abelard, emphasizing those points which will undergo a particularly marked renovation in Rousseau's text and suggesting a historical context within which to place this work of renovation. After identifying the terms of a dialectic in the confrontation between Heloise and Abelard, I will turn to those moments in Rousseau's novel which seem to correspond, in order to suggest how, as in the twelfth-century letters, this dialectic, if such it can be called, proceeds by the elision of the "feminine" negating term.

Let us recall that Heloise is prompted to initiate the exchange of letters with Abelard in order to correct several elements of her portrayal in the *Historia calamitatum*—especially a section of direct discourse in which Abelard attributes to her a certain argument against marriage in general, their marriage in particular. Once the exchange has been begun in this fashion, it continues with her protest of a second misrepresentation: Heloise objects to Abelard's writing to her *as if* she has undergone a conversion upon entering the convent. Instead of Abelard's rhetoric of a radical break, she repeatedly evokes a continuity and reaches for a language which will leave no doubt about the woman who is writing behind the veil. In a final letter, however, having realized that Abelard will refuse any further protest on her part, Heloise agrees, in effect, to silence her complaint and address only questions of monastic rule to the patron of the Paraclete. The issue of her conversion is dropped—and Abelard, once again, addresses her *as if* there were nothing behind her veil.

I want to insist on the two points at which these letters protest a discrepancy between Abelard's veiled representation and Heloise's unveiled one, between her version and his conversion. First of all, it is through this resistance first to marriage and then to the convent that one can discern Heloise's position within the history of those cultural institutions that have, traditionally, defined woman's "place." Second, it is this discrepancy between Heloise and Abelard, the persistence in Heloise's discourse of an unconverted, sexual desire, which in effect will have to undergo a conversion before the renovation of Heloise is complete in its eighteenth-century version. Rousseau, in other words, by writing the *new* Heloise, placed his text in a dialectical relation to its model. This relation is thus one that puts into relief the historical specificity of each work in a way that most of the eighteenth-century prose and verse adaptations of the legend do not (which is one reason they seem so insipid).

The historical context to which I am referring has already been suggested by Paul Zumthor in a passage cited earlier (see Introduction, p. xv) from his essay on Heloise and Abelard. There, it will be recalled, Zumthor characterizes the courtly love topos as the framework that allowed medieval man to ascribe a cultural value to the passions of love, which had, until the end of the eleventh century, remained at the margins of the conceptual universe, "a barbarity which was repulsive to the mind." An analysis of the rhetoric of the correspondence as *courtoise*, however, allows Zumthor to conclude that this text stages a failure of the courtly model to overcome anything but illusory obstacles, reveals, in other words, its redundancy in the face of the real history of separated lovers.

Seen from another point of view, however, the failure which Zumthor analyzes might be described as a remarginalizing of passion, its return to exile. If, as Zumthor also writes, "thanks to [the courtly topos and rhetoric] the relation between the sexes ceased to be either a simple biological function or a spiritual disorder," then it is this notion of a between-the-sexes which is being risked in the courtly language of the letters. At stake is the insertion of this "between" between the accepted limits of the conceptual world—the material and the spiritual, order and disorder. The heterosexual relation, in other words, is being thought both within the parameters of established concepts which have traditionally excluded just such a relation and—at the same time—without reference to those same conceptual limits, which would substitute for the heterosexual difference some rational opposition.

In that version of a relation between the sexes which is the history of Heloise and Abelard, it is possible to read this "between" at a number of different junctures. In a first moment of confrontation, Fulbert's waning feudal order, with its functional, degraded representation of marriage as the marginally and yet only legitimate place for heterosexuality, is challenged by Heloise's (and somewhat more ambiguously, Abelard's) fashioning of a new order outside marriage.[7] This other scene represents itself in terms derived from the courtly poets, as Zumthor has demonstrated. However, a second moment of confrontation follows the first, which had been resolved with Abelard's castration and Heloise's claustration. This second moment is acted out in the correspondence when Heloise resists Abelard's new order of transcendent, spiritual relations. Thus, her letters are set between these two moments of confrontation with, first, Fulbert's model of a functional intercourse between the sexes and, second, Abelard's model of spiritual communion.

The shift from this first moment to the second is best characterized by the shift in the signification of "castration." Fulbert's act of vengeance has meaning through reference to an apparently literal position of the phallus as locus of power. For Abelard, castration becomes a sign—a figure—of God's punishment and grace, and as such establishes a locus of power that is never simply present, literal: the figure of the absent phallus. In Fulbert's brutal gesture, we recognize the effect of a literal avatar of the phallocentric social order, a gesture caught in a moment when, no doubt partly as a result of the confrontation with the rhetoric of obstacle, such literality is no longer sufficient to define the privilege of the phallus. It is from this desperate act that Abelard fashions the new law of castration. Modeled from the remains of an old law, the new one is effective once again in imposing silence on that troubling notion of a between-the-sexes, a place where the phallocentric privilege flounders.

Heloise's text, therefore, falls between Fulbert and Abelard, between the literal reduction of sexual desire to phallic potency and its figural elevation to the beyond of the absent phallus. From its place between these two poles, the text of Heloise's in-difference to one or the other order of castration exposes the continuity of the one in the other despite Abelard's rhetoric of radical discontinuity, rebirth, renewal—that is, of conversion. Her confrontation with the one and the other indicates, in effect, the persistence of a difference within a phallic ordering of the same.

Situating Julie in a similar space between two versions of a same structure brings out an aspect of Rousseau's renovation of Heloise that is overlooked when this material is dismissed as superficial. Like the Heloise of these twelfth-century letters, Julie is positioned at the juncture of one social order which can no longer sustain its claim to legitimate power and another which must succeed to that claim without violence, that is, legitimately. In *The New Heloise*, this articulation is worked out through Julie's passage from her father's archaic law of aristocratic privilege to the renewed order of an enlightened Wolmar, a passage that marks the intermediate term of her passion for Saint-Preux as disorder. The final moment which sets up the new society of Clarens is also the moment at which Rousseau's heroine converts the unconverted remains of Heloise, who only entered Abelard's new kingdom of the absent phallus on the strength of an "as if."

The new society bases its claim for legitimacy on the system with which it guarantees the propriety of its symbolic function—giving things names—and its economic function— giving things value. The legitimacy of the social system, in other words, depends on the legitimate right of its citizens to claim a certain name and a certain property—which is to say, it depends on some guarantee of children's legitimacy within the family.

The question of this relation between the family and the state is one which eighteenth-century social theorists frequently took up and which Rousseau also addressed at the beginning of his *Discourse on Political Economy*. There he notes the error, which these theorists had fallen into, of basing the authority of the state on the natural authority of the father—the error that, for example, gives the title to Robert Filmer's treatise: *Patriarcha; or, The Natural Power of Kings* (1680). The *Discourse,* on the other hand, sets out the distinction between the father's authority and that of the magistrate.

> Although the functions of the father and the first magistrate must aim at the same goal, they proceed along very different paths. Their duty and their rights are so completely distinct in the two cases that to confuse them is to construe false notions of the fundamental laws of society and to fall into errors which are fatal for humankind. While it is true that nature's voice is the best guide for a good father if he is to do his duty well, for the magistrate that same voice is a deceptive guide that works constantly to divert him from his duties and will sooner or later lead him to his ruin and that of the State unless he is restrained by a most sublime virtue. . . . To do well, the former need only consult his heart but the latter becomes a traitor the moment he listens to his. He must treat even his reason with suspicion and follow no other rule but that of the public reason which is the law.[8]

Contrary to what others were maintaining, the concept of "a natural society" that would function on the model of the patriarchal family magnified many times is, in Rousseau's terms, a "false notion" and "a fatal error." While the best fathers "govern" their families according to a natural principle of self-interest, this same principle is anathema to the successful direction of the state, where law rather than nature must determine authority: "Purely arbitrary in its institution, political authority can only be based on conventions and the magistrate can only command others by virtue of laws" (pp. 241–42). The concept of "natural authority" in the state, of the Father King or Patriarchal Magistrate, by revoking the arbitrary principle, clears the way for a tyrannical rather than a legitimate state.

Rousseau nonetheless sets up an analogy between the family and the state, the father and the magistrate. After rejecting the principle of natural authority in the state, however, Rousseau's text can only pose this analogy through the notion of *conventional* authority in the family. "For several reasons that derive from the nature of the thing, the father must be in command in the family" (p. 242). Among the reasons "derived from the nature of the thing" is one which functions to guarantee the production of natural (biological) rather than conventional (social) paternity. "Moreover, the husband must have the right to *inspect* his wife's behavior since it is important for him to have some assurance that the children, whom he is forced to recognize and nourish, do not belong to others than himself. The wife, who has nothing similar to fear, does not have the same right over the husband" (p. 242). The father's position as *inspector* of his wife's conduct is meant to guarantee a genetic link with the children to whom he gives his name. This convention, in other words, is the means by which paternity—and the act of naming which signifies it— seeks to establish itself as a natural, rather than conventional, relation.

A threat to the system guaranteeing natural paternal authority is that a woman, like Heloise, can always act "as if." Her body, with its hidden recesses of generation, can always exchange one man's child for another man's name beyond the reach of the law's inspection. Indeed, that in-spection, or looking into, will always remain on the surface of things, at the level where pretense may pass for sincerity, the natural child for the legitimate one. The subterfuge and the duplicity of the "as if" has the potential to dislocate both the patronymic designation of property and the patrimonial inheritance. By breaking the only "natural" link in the patriarchal chain, the subterfuge in effect exposes the arbi- trary prerogative of the father and thus of the conventions which protect that prerogative.

In Rousseau's novel, this prerogative is menaced with expo- sure and extinction.[9] Saving it requires both that the sterile conventions of the extinguishing order be renewed in a natural relation and that the woman's duplicity—the potential for fal- sifying this "natural" link—be itself exposed, brought to the surface and made visible. This exposure of a woman's subver- sion is a necessary condition for continuity within the legitimate order, and so we will begin our reading of this process with a scene celebrating just such a continuity from one generation of fathers to the next: a marriage ceremony.

Before Julie d'Etange becomes Mme de Wolmar, a revolution takes place which the heroine describes to Saint-Preux as inter- nal: "I thought I felt a sudden, internal revolution. An unknown power seemed to correct all at once the disorder of my feelings and re-establish them according to the laws of duty and nature" (p. 354). This sudden interior revolution intervenes in time to save the public spectacle from the undermining effects of a discrepancy between this woman's outer display and inner disposition. What occurs in that moment, therefore, is the obliteration of the distinct space of the heroine's interiority, or rather its submission to the transcendent principle of "the eternal eye which sees everything" and which can thus compare "[the] hidden will to the spoken response." Before the intervention of this divine organ which has the power to penetrate a woman's surface appearance and assess her internal state, Julie's word was a contradiction that annulled the significance of the public ritual: "In the very moment that I was about to swear eternal fidelity to another, my heart was swearing an eternal love for you. I was led to the temple like an impure victim who spoils the sacrifice in which she is about to be immolated" (p. 353). Rather than this sullied, meaningless sacrifice, Julie's renunciation of her other, silent, promise to Saint-Preux seals the validity of the public performance, guarantees its legitimacy not only for the individual actors but for the spectators as well.

What is displayed here—put on show, brought to the surface—is, indeed, the mechanism of social legitimacy: the inspection of a woman's interior, that hidden, contradictory space where things may not be what they appear. This almost mystical scene in which Julie is converted and thus ceases to conceal a menace to the public order is itself, however, already a conversion of an earlier, violent moment of threat and exposure. As in the history of Heloise and Abelard, the new order of Clarens which is initiated with the heroine's conversion—and which displaces the story of the lovers in the second half of the novel, much as the "Letters of Direction" follow the "Personal Letters" in the twelfth-century correspondence—is the dialectical product of two successive moments of confrontation: the first, a moment of simple negation and violent deadlock; the second, a moment of nonviolent revolution in which the negation is itself negated. We have seen how, in the earlier history, this dialectic is made to work only through Heloise's agreement to write "as if" Abelard's new order of the absent phallus did not, in fact, constitute the same exclusion of her negativity. And we have now also seen how Rousseau converts this "as if" through Julie's vision at her wedding altar of the hidden organ of divine omnipotence, the absent phallus of Abelard's divine order. As a negation of a negation, therefore, this "vision" replaces some earlier apprehension of the face of power. What remains to be seen is this first revelation in violence of the hidden aspect of paternal authority.

Julie's interiority is laid bare in quite another manner through this violence, the beating she suffers at the hands of her father after he has learned of her wish to marry Saint-Preux. Her account of the episode and its aftermath concludes with one of those awkward mimetic moments in this epistolary text when the acts of experiencing an event and writing a letter describing it are made to occupy the same time. In this postscriptum to a letter to Claire, Julie writes: "After my letter was written, I went into my mother's room, but I suddenly felt so ill that I have had to come back to my own bed. I even notice . . . I fear . . . oh, my friend, I fear that my fall yesterday may have a more disastrous result than I thought" (p. 178—ellipses are Rousseau's). Writing in the present, Julie records the moment of a spontaneous abortion, or rather marks this stillbirth with her ellipses. To be sure, in this fashion the hidden proof of Julie's crime against her father's authority is exposed. But the revelations of this letter do not end there. The violence which erupts in this noble Swiss household also exposes the father's law as monstrous, unnatural: "What hellish monsters are these prejudices which degrade the noblest hearts and force nature at every moment to be silent?" writes Julie as she recovers from her injuries. In effect, by attacking his daughter, M. d'Etange denies the natural link which the convention of his authority is meant to guarantee: the father's attachment for the child he knows is legitimately his.

These terms, which we have already encountered in the *Discourse on Political Economy*, will be echoed by Julie in her own discourse on legitimacy, which accompanies the account of her conversion:

> Must not two beings formed of the same blood have between them a stricter analogy and a stronger attachment one for the other? Resembling each other in body as well as soul, do they not have even a greater reason to love each other? Is it then your opinion that one

does no harm if one annihilates or upsets this natural union with a foreign blood, thus altering the principle which supports mutual affection and which should tie together members of a family? [P. 360]

What does it mean, however, when this natural union of father and child is interrupted by the question of the father's legitimacy rather than the child's, when it is the father rather than the child who is unmasked as illegitimate, as a monster who alters "the principle of mutual affection?"

For Etange, the anomaly of his own action has its explanation outside the strict analogy and in the region of "a foreign blood":

As for [Saint-Preux], while I do not question the merit which everyone finds in him, I also do not know if he himself conceived the ridiculous hope of allying himself to me or if someone succeeded in inspiring this idea in him; but . . . you can be sure that I will never accept such a son-in-law. . . . Although I have always felt little sympathy for him, I especially hate him now for the excesses he has forced me to commit and I will never forgive him for my brutality. [Pp. 176–77]

Saint-Preux, by pretending to the position of legitimate son (-in-law) has provoked a father's brutal aggression toward one whom that same father has "a great reason to love." This displacement can itself be explained by recalling that the ultimate victim of the father's excessive violence is the unborn child of Saint-Preux's "ridiculous hope." Illegitimacy—the "foreign blood"—is thus represented at two generational levels of the familial alliance: Saint-Preux as Etange's illegitimate "son," and Julie's illegitimate child. In effect, a displacement occurs between these two so that we see Etange as a father whose brutality "naturally" exposes the child which is not his own.

Julie's encounter with her father, therefore, cannot be wholly inserted into the category of an anomaly, if one means by that a monstrous departure from the natural affection which binds father to child. Inevitably, M. d'Etange's violence gives way to another scene, one which Julie describes in most revealing terms:

[My mother] sat down at one of the corners of the hearth and my father at the other. I was going to get a chair and place myself between them when, holding me by my dress and pulling me towards him without saying a word, he sat me on his lap. This all happened so quickly and as if involuntarily that a moment later he seemed to repent of it. However, I was on his lap and he could not undo what he had done. . . . From time to time I felt his arms press against my sides and heard a barely muffled sigh. I do not know what fear prevented these paternal arms from giving into these sweet embraces. A certain uneasiness that we did not dare overcome placed between this father and his daughter that charming awkwardness that modesty and love place between lovers. . . . I bent my head before his and instantly covered him with my kisses and my tears. . . . Sweet and peaceful innocence, your absence from my heart was all that was lacking from this natural scene to make it the most charming moment of my life! [Pp. 175–76]

Not surprisingly, the editors provide a note to the paragraph I have just quoted at length.[10] Not surprisingly, because, like any note, this one makes the reader turn her attention elsewhere, and somehow one is not surprised that the editors should want to distract us at this point. And, in effect, the note warns us not to read this passage.

This melodramatic scene . . . today sounds *false* to our ears. . . . *It is difficult to see its source in Jean-Jacques's life* [let us reserve this phrase for later comment]. . . . Whereas elsewhere, whenever he speaks of love or friendship, his dream is constructed on the solid base of memory, here it rests on *nothing*. That is the reason for this *forced, artificial* style. Note *in passing* the comparison, which is *in such bad taste*, of the embraces between the Baron and his daughter to those of lovers. Unless one prefers to see in this an intuition of the best-kept secrets of the human heart. [P. 1439]

It is difficult not to read this note as a series of denegations— "false," "nothing," "forced, artificial," "such bad taste"— which finally give way reluctantly ("Unless . . . ") to a formulation of some secret revealed. Let us also note, however (and also "in passing"), that this final formulation seeks to restore the notion that this secret is one "of the best-kept . . . of the human heart." It seems, in other words, that the editors intervene at this moment not to uncover a meaning which Rousseau's text leaves hidden but rather to cover over an idea that that text has had the very bad taste to leave in the open.

This function of the commentary, which intervenes in the text to warn the reader to dismiss or ignore what she has read, is perhaps authorized by Rousseau himself, who prefaced his novel with the warning we have already considered. Could it be that hidden behind Rousseau's apparently quaint caution to chaste girls of the novel's danger is this scene which the editors regard with such discomfort? Is the novel's most corrosive effect, in other words, to be found precisely in its most innocent moment, what Julie herself calls a "natural scene" that was almost—but not quite—"the most charming moment of [her] life?" And if there is danger here, who—or what—is menaced? It is, if we are to continue in the terms of the preface, the chaste girl, the innocent girl, the virgin, whose menacer is (how strange) the father. Inadvertently, however, our editors have allowed us to see another danger, one which apparently still holds a powerful threat in 1964 and which they seek to dismantle with their denegations. It is not the father but rather the girl herself—the reader of the novel—who threatens to upset by exposing, by reading, the system of legitimacy. It is, in other words, not the girl's chastity but the law of the father's desire that is in danger of being interrupted if it is exposed and seen to be factitious, forced. It operates more effectively beneath the cover of law. That cover is blown once desire surfaces, once the father puts his little girl on his knee, presses her flanks with his arms, and gives himself over to her sweet embraces. How else to explain why the editors cannot be heard complaining of the forced or factitious style of the passage relating the baron's assault on his daughter when she has had the temerity to interrupt him in the midst of his invective against Saint-Preux, the man he hardly knows? " 'In heaven's name,' " says Julie, " 'please calm yourself. No man who deserves such scorn will ever present a danger for me' " (p. 174). Where are our editors at this moment to point out the obvious irony—or is it very bad taste?—that as Julie finishes with these words, her father wastes no time becoming the most dangerous man in her life by beating her until she falls at his feet?

What the editors judge to be the bad taste of the scene of paternal tenderness, Julie on the other hand savors as almost the most charming moment of her life. Almost but not quite. She writes: "Sweet and peaceful innocence, your absence from my heart was all that was lacking from this natural scene to make it the most charming moment of my life!" This scene from nature, of the natural union between father and child, is not quite what it could or should be because Julie has lost her innocence. That is, she has known another man's embraces. But that is not all. Because she has known "that charming awkwardness that modesty and love place between lovers," she can formulate in the letter she is writing the comparison which the editors ask us to note in passing, and then, finally, she can conclude that sitting on her father's knee, submitting to his caresses, leaves something to be desired. Julie names that something "innocence," the lack of which produces a slight discrepancy between this scene and the most charming moment of her life. The acknowledgment of a discrepancy between filial affection and an erotic embrace—between a father and a lover—makes Julie guilty of a desire that does not correspond exactly to her father's. In effect, Julie knows (guiltily) that the "natural union" of father and child—this "natural scene"—is produced by a lie, the child's lie that she too desires only the father.

The crime, therefore, is in the knowledge that the father's law rests on the lie by which the child pretends to be "his," the product of his desire alone. It is the lie of the patriarch, whose progeny are vessels which carry only his blood and are marked, therefore, by only his name—thus Julie d'Etange, the only child of the Baron d'Etange, whom Saint-Preux, much earlier in the novel, calls her father's "only hope." This dangerous father would rather kill a child than let it live to bear the name of another, the ridiculously oxymoronic name of Saint-Preux, which joins the spiritual to the everyday or the useful.[11] Saint-Preux, who has conceived "the ridiculous hope of allying himself" to Etange, is the bearer of an impure name precisely because it is double, its hyphen betraying the mixture of blood from two sources. The lover, in other words, is unworthy of Etange because his blood carries the anemic traces of the feminine, "a foreign blood," and allows for the intrusion of the other's child—the child of a woman's deceitful desire—into the line of the patrimony.[12]

The noble name of Etange, on the other hand, has preserved itself from the flow of impurity by the action which it also suggests through the elevation of a common word into a proper name. It is the action of the verb *étancher*—to stop the flow of a liquid, usually blood. *Un cloison étanche* is an absolute separation—for example, between social classes. If we add "between the sexes" to the definition, we identify *cloisons* of the sort that will later set off in the house at Clarens a gynaeceum where women and children alone can be found—with the unique exception, on one occasion, of Saint-Preux, Mme de Wolmar's former lover.

The Baron d'Etanche, however, has also, through the death of his only son, become the Baron d'Etang; his blood having ceased to flow in the veins of a male heir, the name is stagnant, stopped up and menaced with extinction and its own fate of a total *étanchement*, or drying up. Julie is, indeed, the only hope to quench [*étancher*] her father's thirst and let his blood flow into a new gene pool.

To that end, one needs a son-in-law, but one unmarked by the anemic anomie of the feminine, a son-in-law who is of the same blood, and even better, the same name. If there are no more *étangs*, no more homonyms of the father, however, then a synonym is the next best thing—a *mare* for an *étang*, one stagnant pool for another.

Wolmar, the son-in-law, then, is like the father not only because they are of the same class and nearly the same age. He is already allied to Etange by the mark of stagnation, a noble name which survives without fortune, as an anachronism—a prejudice—in an age of revolution. Instead of exile in his own land, Wolmar is designated to take possession of another's patrimony. He is the foreigner whose intervention is made legitimate by the father's *parole*, the foreign blood which, according to the patriarchal logic of the same blood, can appropriate, without crime, the other man's name, the other man's child. Wolmar, the son-in-law, is thus the paradoxical pivot of the patriarchal structure, the hole in the impermeable wall which prevents stagnation even as it preserves the principle of a repetition of the same. By designating Wolmar as legitimate heir, the Baron's word of honor effaces the strangeness of that name—the trace of its difference and its dual genealogy. The man whom Julie must marry does not enter like a thief in the night to steal the only hope of the house of Etange. His appropriation, rather, is a legal *vol*, the exception that makes the rule, a theft by which the owner gets to keep what he loses. The theft disappears in effect with Julie, whose blood is made to flow in an unseen channel between the two stagnant pools. This disappearance leaves, on the surface of things, the legitimate appearance of a repetition of the same, no foreign blood from father to son, *étang* to *mare*.

What is left on the surface by this submerged canalization of the woman's difference is the order of the legitimate society at Clarens, formerly the estate of Etange, which passes, along with Julie, into the hands of Wolmar. The transition from the Baron's vain patriarchy of artifice and prejudice to the more natural order of Wolmar's enlightened management finds its most stunning representation in that center of the moral and aesthetic world of Clarens which is the Elysée garden. As we shall see, however, the garden is not a simple space. Its doubleness—or duplicity—is indeed the *source* of its fertility. As Julie's retreat, therefore, it is also the refuge where the submerged surfaces.[13]

When Saint-Preux is initiated into the secrets of the Elysée, he is slow to grasp the principle behind this garden of illusion, which appears to place, in his characteristically oxymoronic terms, "the ends of the earth at your doorstep" (p. 471). He guesses first that all he sees is natural. "You closed the door, the water was supplied I know not how. Nature did all the rest." Julie patiently corrects him: "It is true that nature did everything, but at my direction. There is nothing here that I did not order." Next, he guesses artifice, exclaiming that if Julie has managed to produce such luxuriance in only seven or eight years, it must have cost at least "two thousand crowns." Again, Julie explains: " 'You overestimate the cost by only two thousand crowns,' she said, 'it cost me nothing.' " Even after repeated demonstrations of this art without artifice, Saint-Preux keeps falling into the contradiction:

> Considering all this, I found it rather odd that one should have
> taken so much trouble to hide from oneself the trouble taken.
> Would it not have been better to do nothing? "In spite of everything
> we have told you," Julie answered me, "you still judge a work by its
> effects and you end up in error. All that you see are wild or hardy
> plants that one need only put in the ground and that then *grow by
> themselves*." [P. 479]

At this point, however, Julie appears herself to have been
taken in by the very illusion she has created, for her denial of
Saint-Preux's remark about the trouble taken to hide *from oneself*
the trouble taken is actually a confirmation of his observation.
When Julie corrects Saint-Preux this time, insisting that he sees
only plants "that grow by themselves," she herself elides that
other element of her garden which, from the outset, Saint-Preux
is least able to account for: the water which is there, as he says, "I
know not how." This element, without which the formerly arid
spot could not have been so transformed ("the grass was rather
dry, the trees somewhat sparse, giving little shade, and there
was no water" [pp. 471–72]) is also the last piece of the puzzle to
be explained to Saint-Preux. " 'I understand now,' I said to Julie,
'everything else but the water that I see everywhere' " (p. 474).
The secret of this secret garden is its water supply, which
appears in myriad forms:

> Here, circulating among the grasses and the flowers in almost
> invisible rivulets, there in larger streams [*ruisseaux*] . . . the mur-
> mur of several small waterfalls . . . and just as many artificial
> springs [*sources*]. Several trickles climbed by means of siphons onto
> rough terrain and bubbled as they fell back down.

Finally, all these water paths lead to the basin:

> I found all the water joined to form a pretty stream [*ruisseau*]. . . .
> Almost at the extremity of the enclosure [*enceinte*] was a small
> basin . . . and the last station of this precious, well-tended water.
> [P. 475]

Why does Julie herself obfuscate the necessity of the water
when she protests that the plants of the Elysée grow, as it were,
"by themselves"? Consider the source of these waters:

> "They come from over there," she continued, pointing in the direc-
> tion of her garden terrace. "It is the same stream [*ruisseau*] that

supplies, at such expense, the garden water-jet which no one cares for. M. de Wolmar does not want to destroy it out of respect for my father, who had it built. Still, with what pleasure we come everyday to this grove to watch the course of the water that we hardly even look at in the garden. The water-jet puts on its show for strangers, the stream here runs for us." [P. 474]

In this device of garden engineering, which siphons water from one point to another, here from Etange's water-jet to the Wolmars' basin, we recognize the figure which governs the transition from father to son-in-law, *étang* to *mare*. The showy and expensive pretension of the water-jet—a remnant of another age which survives only out of the respect due a father—has, by means of a subterfuge, resurfaced in this "simple and mean place" (p. 480), emblem of the economy of the new order of Clarens. Julie gives no details of how this transfer was engineered, leaving us to guess that what is thus covered over, perhaps, is an underground channel. What is clear, however, is that this water from the father's source does not end up unchanged in the basin of its destination.

It is true that I have joined it with water from the public spring which was flowing into the lake over the main road, thus making it dangerous for passers-by and not doing anyone any good. It made a bend at the far end of the grove between two rows of willows. I have included them in my enclosure and I circulate the same water by other paths. [P. 474]

Thus, the excess of the father's pure artifice has been joined to the excess of a natural source—the public spring—run awry in its rush toward the common level of the lake. The Elysée is the joint product—the child, so to speak—of a subterfuge which preserves a father's vanity and harnesses and encloses a gravitational flow. Once again, it is important to remark the doubling which takes place, the fact that the Elysée is supplied by two different sources.[14]

As soon as Saint-Preux is given this key to the Elysée's almost tropical lushness, he notices that, in effect, "it had only been a matter of intertwining these waters economically, dividing and reuniting them as the case may be, preserving the incline as much as possible in order to prolong the circuit and procure for oneself the murmur of several little waterfalls." The garden, in other words, is constructed as a detour, a serpentine path which prolongs, as long as possible, the gravitational descent of the stream toward the lake. Artifice and nature are thus once again represented in a conjunction through this description of a harnessing of the laws of gravity, derived, on the one hand, from the water-jet—a purely artificial overpowering of gravitational attraction—and, on the other, from the public spring, that natural force that proceeds with little heed to the needs of society.

As an allegory for the transformation of society at Clarens, the Elysée invites those who pass through to contemplate the family structure that sustains it in terms of the natural law of gravity given an order. That is, the Wolmar family occupies a place similar to the basin in their secret garden—at a level somewhere between the wasteful attempt to overcome gravity of the water-jet and the lake into which nature directs its flow. The artful *enceinte* at Clarens exists as a detour—a *ménagement*—of gravity's law, the law of falling, gravid bodies (from *gravitas*: weight, heaviness, pregnancy, authority, majesty). L'Elysée, "by dividing and reuniting them as the case may be," controls the flow of these two streams into each other and manages the fertility of the inhabitants.

As a space of resolution where once again Saint-Preux observes that "one finds nothing . . . that does not relate the agreeable to the useful" (p. 470), the Elysée offers a spatialized figure of the *femme (comme) enceinte*, the woman as enclosure but also the woman enclosed and made pregnant. What Saint-Preux is given to see is the concrete result of Julie's conversion, in which a hidden, interior space of potential deception was laid bare and thus renewed. The garden is a spatial representation of the moment when Julie became Mme de Wolmar, which is to say, the new Julie—and the new Heloise.

Yet, is that other name for the heroine not somewhere to be read in the name of the garden, which Rousseau spells *Elisée*, a near anagram? But if this garden bears the name of Heloise, then that name has been elided and the elision has taken out the "o." The garden of *l'eau élidée*? The water which is everywhere evident has been brought by Julie's ingenious subterfuge, her subterranean channeling of water from two sources. And yet it is, as we have seen, the element which is itself elided when she delivers the secret of these plants which spring autochthonously from the soil, by themselves. The dialectical resolution would seem to have its only reality at this level of an elisional discourse which leaves out precisely what is most evident. The garden is thus also the space where the elision resurfaces, where what has been left out of the line of inheritance from father to son (-in-law) reappears. Wolmar tells Saint-Preux that "Julie began [the garden] a long time before her marriage and almost right after the death of her mother" (p. 472). According to this chronology, the garden is that which has sprung up in the place of the elided term of patriarchy.

Naming the garden—giving it a place within the proper and propertied realm of discourse—works to disguise the elision, to cover over what is left out. Although it is Julie herself who has chosen the name *Elisée* for her secret garden, it is finally Wolmar who gives it its meaning. Saint-Preux, who remembers the groves of her father's estate, questions Julie about the need for this other garden. Julie, unable to answer with a reason, blushes. Wolmar interrupts to remind Saint-Preux that he is being indiscreet, that Mme de Wolmar never sets foot now in these groves for reasons which he can guess (it was there that Julie gave Saint-Preux his first kiss). He ends with this warning to the intruder in the garden: "Learn respect for the ground on which you stand. It has been planted by the hands of virtue" (p. 485).

When Saint-Preux returns alone to the garden the following day, it is as if that phrase had in the meantime been engraved above the entrance, like the inscription above the entrance to Dante's Hell. Returning to the *Elisée* with the anticipation of finding Julie "everywhere just as she is deep within [his] heart," it is instead Wolmar's last word—virtue—which he encounters everywhere.

> Entering the Elisée in this frame of mind, I suddenly recalled the last word that M. de Wolmar said to me yesterday at more or less the same place. The memory of this single word changed on the spot the whole state of my soul. I thought I saw the image of virtue where I had come seeking that of pleasure. [P. 486]

Although it is Julie's own key which has let Saint-Preux into the garden this time, it is still Wolmar who unlocks what he will see there. This master key gives access to more than the superfluous, visible pleasures of the garden. It is the word which unveils the hidden interior of meaning, the meaning of *Elisée*:

> Everything, including the name Elisée, corrected the distortions [*écarts*] of my imagination. . . . In a certain manner, it painted for me the *interior* of the woman who had chosen it. I thought that if one's conscience were troubled one would never have chosen such a name. I said to myself, "Peace reigns in her heart as it does in the asylum [*asile*] she has named." [P. 487]

Like a pictograph, the name *Elisée* represents that terrain of speculation which is a woman's interior. For Julie to retreat to this asylum, then, is to find refuge in the space left by the elision of her other name, its subsumption to the law of patronymy. As a kind of loophole, an asylum within the law, the *Elisée* gives refuge to the outlaw. The *Asilée*, the woman protected, but no less confined, *enceinte* in the loophole. Beyond its limits, where the law operates without exception, the *élidée* Hel(o)ise, the *asilée*, is in danger of another fall.

The basin of the Elysée, as we have already observed, is placed at a level somewhere between the water-jet and the lake. Its "between-ness" constitutes a safe haven for Julie along the line of descent from father to son, which has already once caused her to fall. Along the temporal axis of the novel as well, then, the Elysée is evoked as between—between the fall before the father's violence (like the water-jet the product of an anachronistic prejudice) and the fall into the lake.[15] This second fall, which saves a child's life, is linked, by means of substitution, to the first, which precipitates the other (and the other's) child's death.[16] The line connecting these two moments in the novel is one which follows the natural path of descent from a father's honor to a son's life, a life which emerges from the leveling force of the lake. Inexorable natural law—the law of gravity, which describes the flow of water from the father's water-jet to the level of the lake—appears in this sequence as the coefficient of the paternal law which describes the woman's fall as prelude to her disappearance underground.

I want to follow one more detour, not only "to prolong the stroll" (p. 479) as one would do in Julie's garden, but also "to prolong my pleasure"[17] as does the autobiographer Rousseau when he returns to that earthly paradise which was his childhood—before the fall—and to the garden he once tended so carefully. We turn back now in order to pick up the editor's remark cited earlier which, as we observed when we first encountered it, functions as a kind of detour sign for the reader and which we set aside until we could read it in its fullest context: "It is difficult to see its *source* in Jean-Jacques's life" (p. 1439). This remark, one will recall, occurred in the note dismissing as "forced, artificial" the scene of reconciliation between Julie and her father. There, the editor seems puzzled by the lack of resemblance between the Baron d'Etange and Isaac Rousseau, Jean-Jacques's father, at least as he is portrayed in the *Confessions*, and concludes that "judging by the rapid portrait in the *Confessions*, his father was for him an indulgent pal and an extravagant educator, neither too strict nor overly affectionate." I would like to suggest that Julie's relation to her father does have a "source in Jean-Jacques's life," one, however, which has been covered over.

In book 1 of the *Confessions*, after Rousseau recounts the disillusioned departure from Bossey in the aftermath of an unjust accusation, his narration cannot resist the temptation to return there and to recall one or two pleasant episodes. The narrative sequence at this point thus tends to disregard its own division of this period into pre- and postlapsarian frames, differentiated by the experience of an injustice: "That was the end of my peaceful childhood. . . . We remained at Bossey for several more months. We lived there as the first man is portrayed, living still in an earthly paradise but having ceased to find pleasure in it" (p. 21). This ambiguous, lame-duck period seems to dislocate the neat distinction of before and after the fall, and when Rousseau returns to fill in this period of his life with more anecdotes, they are not situated in relation to the crime dividing the stay at Bossey. This is worth noting, since the episode which is most elaborately recounted concerns a crime and its discovery by M. Lambercier. It is, moreover, a crime whose authorship, this time at least, Rousseau takes pleasure in claiming. In fact, the episode is introduced in the mode of self-indulgence, the author imagining for this purpose a reader whose wishes he must dismiss if he is to tell the story.

> I am well aware that the reader does not really need to know all this, but me, I need to tell it to him. If only I dared to tell him all the little anecdotes from this happy time that, when I remember them, still give me a pleasant shiver. Five or six especially . . . let us compromise. I will spare you all five, but I want one of them, one only, provided that I may tell it with as much detail as possible, in order to prolong my pleasure. [Pp. 21–22—ellipses are Rousseau's]

Having struck this bargain, Rousseau hesitates before choosing which anecdote he will indulge himself in telling, like a child before a penny candy display who has only one cent to spend. He teasingly alludes to what he imagines would please his selfish reader—the story of Mlle Lambercier's behind, "which, through an unfortunate tumble at the bottom of a field, was neatly spread before the King of Sardinia as he passed." In the place of this story of a woman's fall and exposure, a woman whom the author loved "like a mother, perhaps more," Rousseau announces, in mock heroic style, "the great tale of the walnut tree . . . the terrible tragedy." The story that will finally be neatly spread out before the reader is one which, in effect, covers over the mother's humiliation. What is more, it substitutes for a situation in which the autobiographical subject was an alarmed spectator another scene that figures the subject as amused actor.

> [The anecdote] of the walnut tree is more amusing for me, who had a role in it, while I was only a spectator of the somersault. I confess that I found no reason to laugh at an accident which, although comic in itself, caused me to feel alarmed for a person whom I loved like a mother, perhaps more. [P. 22]

Finally, because the narrative sets up the sequence of a son's alarm before the spectacle of a mother's unveiling followed by a tale of the boy's heroic imitation of a father, it would seem that the narrator's pleasure in this sequence derives from a retelling of his own happy Oedipal scenario.

But the "great tale of the walnut tree" is the story of a subterfuge, that is, an underground passage by means of which the subject eludes the father's self-perpetuating order. The elements of that story are well known: M. Lambercier's walnut tree is planted with solemn ceremony that is compared both to a baptism ("the two pensioners were its godparents") and to a military conquest ("we arrived . . . at the very natural idea that it was worthier to plant a tree in the garden than a flag in the breach"). This "very natural idea" begets a desire: "We resolved to procure this glory for ourselves and not share it with anyone." The "stately walnut tree" thus begets a little willow cutting that the boys plant in the same fashion as they had seen M. Lambercier do, not forgetting to make a basin around the foot of their "tree" to hold water. But getting water to the tree is precisely the problem, for to be seen carrying it would be to give away their secret garden. The solution that was found is announced in the form of a maxim which invokes the necessity of a mother: "Finally, necessity, the mother of industry, suggested to us an invention with which we could preserve our tree and ourselves from certain death." Note that although a mother resurfaces here as the necessary link between the father's basin and the son's, and as that which preserves from "a certain death," this term surfaces only to suggest an underground solution—a hidden canal or aqueduct siphoning the needed water from the parent tree.

The construction of the secret channel is recounted in precise, overflowing detail.

> We dug our basin deeper in order to create the right slope for the water. We cut the bottoms of boxes into small, narrow slats, some of which we placed flat and end to end while others we set on an angle at either side on top of these. Thus, they made a triangular canal for our conduit. At the entrance, we placed little pieces of fine wood in a pattern which formed a kind of grillwork or screen that caught silt and stones without stopping the flow of water. We carefully covered over our work with well-packed earth. [P. 23]

Rousseau here indulges himself in a description which, more than any other moment in the same anecdote, represents the superfluous—unnecessary—part of the story he is supposed to be telling. "I am well aware that the reader does not really need to know all this, but me, I need to tell it to him." Just as the construction of this aqueduct has its place as a necessary invention which saves the child's desire from the father's jealously exclusive order, the re-construction of the anecdote makes a place for the necessity of "me, I, to tell." In the construction of the aqueduct, then, there already figures the necessity of the re-construction of this other subject which doubles, and undermines, the august singularity of the paternal autochthon. While the subterranean invention of the canal is set in a hidden space between two terms, the walnut and the willow—but as well a desire and its realization, or a crime and its discovery—the superfluity of that "between" is nonetheless the ingenious ground from which "me, I" needs to speak. For that reason, the subject of the anecdote in which Rousseau indulges himself is neither Mlle Lambercier's comically exposed *derrière* nor M. Lambercier's augustly proud tree, but an artful device that works below the surface, effective because covered over, as called for in the other maxim that directs this work: "Omnia vincit labor improbus."

There is, however, another sense in which the aqueduct anecdote is a conduit. By its interposition we are led from the clever little architect at Bossey to the serene designer of Elysée, the gardener who disguises herself in those willows "which grow by themselves." Likewise, a link is established between the walnut tree and the water-jet, both symbols of ceremonial paternal glory. Diverting the element that sustains that glory into other channels demands a "labor improbus"—a dishonest work—that produces the subject of the autobiographer's art no less than and no differently than that of the novelist's. The aqueduct—the channel of duplicity—connects, finally, Rousseau to the figure of the woman forced underground.

5 / DETOUR SIGNS
Les Liaisons Dangereuses

I notice . . . that I have written a volume, having projected to write only a word.

The Marquise de Merteuil

This letter has led me farther than I expected.

The Vicomte de Valmont

 OUR reading of Rousseau's novel follows the path of a double detour which is both the deflection that at several crucial moments menaces the straight line of inheritance from father to son and the principle of prolongation which preserves life in the garden. In either mode, the detour maintains an underground relation to the woman who both relieves a stagnation in the father's identity and threatens to drain its vital substance. Uncovering the various subterfuges and secret conduits that run throughout the novel—and beyond—is therefore a work of excavation.

In Choderlos de Laclos's only novel, *Les Liaisons Dangereuses*, the detour has surfaced; indeed, it constitutes the readable surface of the text. If, that is, we can still call *readable* a text which is almost entirely constructed out of such deviations from the sense of it all. As a letter-fiction or a textual field of meaning delimited by the two alternating poles of sender and receiver, *Les Liaisons* adopts as its condition of possibility of meaning the doubleness or duplicity that also allows for, even necessitates, the possibility of a deviation of that meaning from the addressed destination. Reading this novel cannot be a simple matter, since a letter arrives, if it arrives, only in its (possibly) detoured form, having taken (perhaps) a borrowed path.[1]

While any letter-novel adopts the same condition of possibility/impossibility, *Les Liaisons* offers its readers relatively little protective cover behind which to forget or ignore the text's possible duplicity. To begin with, the device of the frame, which could serve to contain the careening deviations of the letters, is rendered useless precisely because it is two-sided: the editor's preface is itself preceded by a publisher's foreword that advises us, ironically it would seem, to disregard the editor's claim for the authenticity of the letters. And at the other limit of the text, a similar dismantling of the limit occurs: the word "End" is succeeded by an ambiguous note from the publisher which alludes to a possible continuation of the adventures of Merteuil and Cécile. A simple effect of this tampering with the frame from within the fiction is the erosion which overtakes the attempt to settle upon the limits of the text from without. By encompassing with his own introduction and notes those which are part of the text of the novel, the modern editor (Yves Le Hir, for example, for the Garnier edition) is functioning at least in part in a mode already figured by the fictional editor, so that one reads this gesture, which presumes fixed terms on the object, as already inscribed from within the object. The job of editing these letters, if only insofar as it requires setting the terms of a beginning and an end, is a very tricky business. At these limits, no less than in the main body of the novel, something risks going astray.

In a certain sense, Rousseau's novel describes the detour as the connecting principle of the epistolary form, that from which and by which the letters proceed. Significantly, it is the principle to which Julie refers in the long letter of recapitulation that marks a break in the text by offering a summary of the events thus far. Recalling the first moments of their passion, Julie writes to Saint-Preux:

> I knew my heart and judged myself to be lost at your first
> word. . . . I tried vainly with a feigned coldness to keep you distant
> in the *tête-a-tête*. This constraint itself was my downfall: you *wrote*.
> Instead of throwing your first letter into the fire or carrying it to my
> mother, I dared to open it. That was my crime, and the rest necessarily followed. [Pp. 341–42]

At the two crucial moments which are the writing and the reading of the first letter, Julie retrospectively points to a fatal divergence from the straight and narrow. In the first moment,

writing bypasses the constraint imposed on the spoken exchange. In the second moment, reading deflects the letter from
its direct path into the fire or into the mother's hands. Neither of
these moments, however, is a simple deviation.

By the terms of Saint-Preux's first letter, what must be re-
strained is precisely the passion that threatens to lead the
pedagogical exchange off its reasoned course.[2] But at the same
time as the letter he writes circumvents this constraint, it also
offers itself as a shortcut back to the path of virtue. He writes: "I
can see, Mademoiselle, only one way to get out of the difficulty
[*embarras*] I am in. . . . Show my letter to your parents; have me
thrown out of your house. . . . I cannot flee you on my own" (p.
32). The solution which Saint-Preux proposes here is precisely
the road not taken that Julie regrets: showing this letter to her
mother or throwing it into the fire. One way or the other, Julie's
analysis, which situates her crime at the moment the novel
opens, suggests that it is only in some region before the letter
that she was not already covered with the shame of her passion
for Saint-Preux. Destroying the letter or bringing it home to
mother are finally equivalent means of short-circuiting the
reading of the letter and of remaining therefore in that prefic-
tional region before the crime. Reading it, however, Julie engages the mechanism of the double-bind, that is, the *written*
imperative *not to read* (to show the letter to her mother) which in
order to obey she must disobey. Once engaged, the double-bind
will continue to proliferate the letters and thus widen the gap
which separates Julie from her pretextual innocence and from the
possibility of a return to the mother.

This recapitulation is a necessary digression in our approach
to *Les Liaisons* since Laclos, to a certain extent, has duplicated
Rousseau's novel in his own. This relation is set out already on
the title page, which includes an epigraph chosen from the first
preface to *Julie*. " 'I have seen the morality of my time and I have
published these letters.' " This quotation in a changed context
produces an equivocation in the referent of "these letters," a
forced ambiguity through which one collection of letters may be
substituted for the other. In that switch, however, *Julie*'s positive
moral example is siphoned off in the direction of *Les Liaisons*'s
negative example. This embezzlement or diversion of funds

already suggests the (mis)use which Merteuil makes of *Julie* as a source in her preparations for the seduction of young Belleroche: " . . . I read a chapter of *Le Sopha*, a letter from *The New Heloise*, and two fables of La Fontaine to record the different tones I wanted to adopt."[3] Just as Merteuil's practice of seduction results in a *détournement de mineur*, Laclos's (mis)appropriation of Rousseau's novel swerves it off course on an aberrant trajectory.

Yet the digression which is *Les Liaisons* in its relation to *Julie* would not be possible if that first novel were not already operating in the indirect mode of the letter. If we restore the epigraph to its original context, we find that it is within just such a departure from a straight moral lesson that Rousseau inscribed his novel. "Just as large cities need the theatre, corrupt people need novels. I have seen the morality of my time and I have published these letters. If only I had lived in a time when I would have been obliged to *throw them into the fire!*" (p. 5). The oblique path of the moralist / novelist, however, who instead of burning such letters sends them on for others to read, announces very precisely that other deviation figured in the letters: to wit, Julie's failure to throw Saint-Preux's first letter into the fire. Through its tangential address to "the morality of [its] time," in other words, the letter-novel always risks going astray, falling into the wrong hands. The check on this potential for deviation is, as we know, Rousseau's warning in the same preface to the chaste girl to close his book before it is too late.

A closer comparison between this preface to *Julie* and the editor's preface to *Les Liaisons* would suggest that, once again, Laclos took Rousseau as a model. One finds the same apology for the faulty style and the same modest prediction that such a work will have only a limited appeal. There is, however, one noteworthy divergence from Rousseau's presentation of his work. The author of the preface to *Les Liaisons* in effect doubles the potential for the dangerous drift of these letters into the wrong hands by warning "the youth *of both sexes*" of the abuse ("always so close to the good way") into which such letters could lead. He concludes: "Far from recommending this work to youth, it seems to me very important to divert [*éloigner*] young people from reading anything of this kind" (p. 5). We have here an initial indication of how Laclos's novel works to compound the original mistake that Julie identifies with the reading of a first letter and that leads Rousseau to single out the "chaste girl" from the audience of readers. By doubling the abuse of the letter, Laclos removes the only check on that abuse, for the check is grounded finally in the sexual opposition. Once the concept of outside-the-book (or before-the-letter) is no longer defined with reference to sexual difference, every other differentiation that operates within the space of the letters—writer/reader, sender/receiver, seducer/seduced—is set adrift on a course that threatens to take with it the very shores of anchored stability. No chaste girl can find a place either inside or outside such writing.[4]

When we write, then, that Laclos's letter-fiction duplicates Rousseau's, that too must be understood in two senses. That is, there is both a repetition of certain features of the intrigue and a deflection of these features into the misleading orbit of the double. The couple Cécile/Danceny, for example, are but a more naive, more prosaic version of the couple Julie/Saint-Preux. Like the Swiss lovers, the Parisian innocents discover desire in the pedagogical situation and begin a correspondence in the same fashion as Rousseau's characters. Once begun, however, that correspondence rebounds by means of a set of reduplications. First, Merteuil, acting as Cécile's other mother, acquires the girl's confidence precisely by authorizing the continuation of her exchange with Danceny. Valmont enters at an analogous moment to reinstate that exchange after it has been interrupted by Mme de Volanges (which is to say, by Merteuil). Valmont's liaison role soon yields to his position as Danceny's proxy with Cécile, and the exchange of letters is briefly short-circuited by a sexual exchange with the mailman. For the series to be complete, it only remains for Merteuil to seduce Danceny away from Cécile, in the guise this time, however, of the young girl's substitute.

This turning aside of the source of the letter-fiction in *Julie* remains, nevertheless, a pretext for a far more disruptive trajectory which binds together Valmont, Merteuil, and Tourvel and propels them beyond a fail-safe point. It is within this other trajectory that the potential for the letter to go astray comes closest to dismantling the structural oppositions which support the reader's capacity to follow and arrive at the drift of the text. Yet, if one is not to short-circuit the reading of these letters, it is this possibility of being set adrift that has to be engaged.

Already in her third letter to Valmont, Merteuil compares his delaying tactic in the project to seduce Tourvel to a side trip, a slow journey along back roads. "But you, who are no longer yourself [*qui n'êtes plus vous*], you are behaving as if you were afraid of succeeding. Since when do you travel by short spurts and on side roads [*des chemins de traverses*]? My friend, when you want to *arrive*, fast horses and the main road!" (p. 25). What is at stake in this excursion, as Merteuil here reminds him, is Valmont's reputation as a seasoned adventurer on the high road of seduction. Indeed, her impatience with his overdue arrival has initiated the correspondence between the two libertines, since the first letter to the Vicomte opens with an appeal for a speedy return: "Come back, my dear Vicomte, come back. What are you doing, what could you be doing at your old aunt's house? . . . Leave right away, I need you. . . . You will receive this letter tomorrow. I demand that tomorrow, at seven o'clock in the evening, you be here with me" (pp. 9–10). In effect, Valmont defers this rendezvous until almost the end of the novel—four months of narrative time or almost 150 letters later—by which time, of course, he has missed his appointment. In that space of his deferral, Valmont is between engagements: not yet and no longer the seducer of Tourvel, no longer and not yet Merteuil's lover. The interval of this novel is that of an interim between two points of arrival, two projects of seduction, two women—which is to say, two correspondences. Thus, in order to describe the effects of jealousy within this triangle—or any other effects—one cannot cut short the letter's course, since it is there that something gets sent off in another direction.

It is not long before Merteuil is warning Valmont of the danger of writing. "But the real blunder is having let yourself write [*vous être laissé aller à écrire*]. I defy you to foresee now where this may lead you" (p. 67). If Merteuil here sounds a warning of the possible deviations which the letter may impose on the course of Valmont's seduction, it is not only because they could delay consummation. What is potentially more dangerous is the space now created for a different response, one which is other than the one requested. Her own letter continues with the counterpoint of the spoken tactic where this interval all but disappears and where "the presence of the loved object makes us desire to be conquered." She closes with a final piece of advice: "Listen to me, Vicomte: you have been asked to stop writing. Take advantage of this request to repair your mistake [*faute*] and wait for a chance to speak" (p. 68).

Valmont's reply to this letter is deceptively simple:

> Why go to such lengths to prove what everyone knows? To go quickly in love, it is better to speak than to write. . . . Whatever the case may be, a lawyer would tell you that the principle does not apply to the question at hand. In effect, you presume that I have the choice between speaking and writing, *which I do not.* [P. 69]

On a first level, Valmont's reply recalls the pragmatic constraints of his situation. Ever since his first declaration, Tourvel has avoided the *tête-à-tête*. Like Saint-Preux, therefore, Valmont is prompted to write his first letter in order to get around this obstacle in his path. On another level, however, the logic of this moment is one in which the concepts of project as a straight course to the object and of detour as (potentially) a drifting away from that object are confused. What Valmont signals here as his own lack of choice is the necessity of the detour *within* the project if it is to arrive at its goal. His procedure at this moment, in other words, must—in order to proceed—include the possibility of the letter's loss of direction.

Merteuil's reminder of proper procedure in such situations, on the other hand, figures something like an irresistible presence to itself of the seducer's project in a flawless performance that combines intonation, tears, gesture, and tender looks. "That is why," she writes, "the most mediocre play, which one could never bring oneself to read, never misses having an effect in the theater" (p. 68). Merteuil's criticism of Valmont's performance, however, calls up finally an image of a sovereign actor whose impeccable *jeu* leaves one speechless, defenseless. Her logic, which clearly sorts out a choice between speaking and writing and between, therefore, a faultless and a deficient execution of a project, is the same which leads another of Valmont's critics to imagine, even if only in passing, "perfect evil." "No one could have resisted perfect evil [*le mal parfait*]: a Valmont who does not write letters could not have been unmasked."⁵ The concept of the choice between writing and not writing, in other words, is the concept of a project thought in its perfection, what in this context would occupy the irresistibly seductive place of "le mâle parfait," the perfect male—man, that is, before the (fault of the) letter. Thus, the blunder or *maladresse* with which Merteuil reproaches Valmont is given this other sense of something lacking within a man's project to have a woman, a fault which is marked by the address of a letter.⁶

Yet, when Merteuil urges Valmont to employ another kind of *adresse*—that of the skill or dexterity of the combatant—she does so in a mode which in effect substitutes for the "attack" on Tourvel the example of an attack on Merteuil herself. That is, by advising Valmont to adopt a change of tactic, her letter at the same time urges him to use a change of address—to turn and return his attentions to her.

> For myself, I confess, the thing that flatters me most is a hearty, well-mounted attack . . . which maintains an air of violence even in those things which we concede, and which flatters skillfully [*avec adresse*] our two distinct passions, the glory of defense and the pleasure of defeat . . . and sometimes it even happens that I give myself up, simply as reward. Just as in the ancient tournaments, beauty gave the prize for valor and skill [*adresse*]. [P. 25]

It is this letter, letter 10, which continues with an intimate description of Merteuil's preparation for a night with her current lover, that provokes Valmont into requesting just such a return to the marquise's favor. Merteuil will respond with a contract whose terms are simple: she agrees to become Valmont's mistress again but only as the prize for his eventual victory over Tourvel.

It is clear to any reader of the novel that the exchange which takes place at this moment between Valmont and Merteuil is highly significant for the unraveling of the plot. What may be easily overlooked, however, in this re-destination of Valmont's project, is a small confusion that accompanies that exchange and that is already perhaps a signal of another, far more consequential, disturbance later in their correspondence. Briefly, letter 20,

which contains Merteuil's proposal for the renewal of their
liaison, goes somewhat astray. A note from the "editor" indicates that before Valmont received it, he had already sent two
more letters to Merteuil (numbered 21 and 23), the second of
which discloses that he has written to Tourvel.[7] In the exchange
which then ensues about this blunder, Valmont neglects to acknowledge receipt of the contract. In fact, he does not refer to this
promise until letter 58 and then not again until letter 99, on what
he thinks is the eve of Tourvel's capitulation. "Finally, my lovely
one, I will arrive without delay at your door to demand that you
keep your word. You have no doubt not forgotten what you
promised me after my victory?" (p. 229). By this time, of course,
and just as Merteuil had warned, Valmont's correspondence
with Tourvel has led him way off course. The (double) arrival he
announces for the next day will not take place as foreseen. Again,
Valmont misses his connection and the fiction continues.

If we ask, however, at what point the project to seduce Tourvel
and win Merteuil's favor goes awry, the answer would have to be
duplex—would have to recognize, that is, that already at the
outset a difference bifurcates the point of departure. In that
simple notion of the desire to arrive another desire is already
crossing it like a *chemin de traverse*, since Valmont's progress
toward Tourvel is also a progress toward Merteuil in the terms of
that contract which we have deferred reading until now:

> As soon as you have had your beautiful, pious woman, and have
> furnished me with proof, come and I am yours. You know, how-
> ever, that for important affairs, the only proof is a written one. In
> this fashion, on the one hand, I will be a reward instead of being a
> consolation. This idea pleases me more. On the other hand, your
> success will be sweeter as it will become a means of infidelity. So
> come, come as soon as you can and bring me the token of your
> triumph, just like our brave knights who deposited at the feet of
> their lady the brilliant spoils of their victory. [P. 42]

In effect, Merteuil proposes a circular trajectory for Valmont's
project, one which will bring it all back home. For the major part
of the novel, this circularity, whereby the seduction of Tourvel is
posed as merely a pretext for the return to Merteuil, disguises a
double inscription which is no less duplicitous on the one hand

than the other. Valmont is engaged on a path in the course of which he risks losing his identity as a skillful seducer in the address to Tourvel. On the other hand, therefore, he steers directly toward his object by referring to that source of his identity in the correspondence with Merteuil.

The circular notion of the return, by short-circuiting the address of the letter back to a point before the novel opens, also disguises the reader's engagement in the text. It sets out a model of reading as a bypassing of the text, a reading, in other words, of an impossible origin of the book. It is that region alluded to in an editor's note about the beginning of Valmont's and Merteuil's liaison: "Since this affair was altogether ordinary and since it was also quite anterior to the period of these letters, we thought it best to eliminate [*supprimer*] this whole correspondence" (p. 10). The suppression referred to here leaves the beginning of the relation between the two principle correspondents in the space of an origin which is outside the text, preexisting and thereby causing the letters which one reads. This causality is given the minimal necessary support when the editor points out that in this first liaison one would find the *pretext* for the revenge on Gercourt, a motif that explains the intrigue of the novel, excepting, of course, Valmont's seduction of Tourvel. It is this exception which the structure of circularity attempts to reappropriate by describing a trajectory in which the end—the goal—is also a return to a pretextual, preliteral beginning.

Of course, the editor's decision not to include this earlier correspondence has a practical explanation. The book has to begin somewhere. This constraint has nonetheless the effect of veiling the source of the novel's peripeties. Since the reader can only defer to the editor's better judgement in this matter, the hidden origin is allowed to function as that cache of meaning which explains the letters from a point outside their crisscrossing circuits. The novel's sense is thus held in reserve and the reader is encouraged subliminally, that is, from the margins at the bottom of the page, to direct his/her course through the series of letters back to this point which cannot be read. The text's reader is thus given a way out of the maze that is a shortcut around the dangers ahead.

For an idea of why one might agree to take such a shortcut,

consider the conclusions of two critics who have little difficulty imagining what transpired between Valmont and Merteuil during their first liaison. Each would seem to want to lift the veil thrown over the letters at the outset in order to set straight the record of the power balance between the two former lovers—to put things back where they belong. Their efforts, therefore, will focus on Merteuil's fraud, her pretension to have more than she is entitled to. The title chosen by one of these readers, Aram Vartanian, already announces rather precisely the mystification he will uncover: "The Marquise de Merteuil: A Case of Mistaken Identity." We quote from the conclusion of this study of Merteuil's false androgyny:

> The Marquise is not, as she imagines, Valmont's match. Her superiority, more apparent that real, results in part from her exceptional talents, but especially from her assumed double role, which puts at her disposal, in dealing with others, the weapons peculiar to both sexes, a portion of which remain, moreover, secret weapons for her unsuspecting victims [. . .]. In the *dénouement* that follows, the proper role of each sex is re-affirmed with a vengeance.[8]

Similarly, Georges Daniel does not hesitate to read from a position before the letter of the text, from which point it is possible for him to conclude that "by a totally free and finally gratuitous decision [Merteuil] has chosen to wear a mask. She cultivates the art of dissimulation without necessity."[9] Beneath her veils, in other words, the marquise has nothing to hide. Both of these readers follow a circular course through the novel back to an unwritten scenario where roles are properly distributed between man and woman, the strong and the weak, the one who has it and the one who has nothing.

Valmont, however, is in a different position. If he accepts the conditions of circularity and the possibility of a return to an origin, then it can only be in order to better disguise that dispersion of the letter which he engages with the other hand. Thus, the circular strategy is a *garde-fou*, a cautionary mechanism which, like Ariadne's thread, allows him to follow all the angles in the other's labyrinth with the assurance that he can return to his point of departure. In effect, by superimposing the return to Merteuil and to an original source of identity on the uncharted terrain of the address to Tourvel, Valmont contrives to have the one in the other, to "have," that is, Merteuil in Tourvel, to "have," therefore, his identity, but as singular, detached from its source. The address to Tourvel thus also operates as a safety device which guards against a return, once and for all, without recourse, to the origin of identity in the other.[10] It is as double that Valmont can judge his project to be sublime, a singular departure from that repetition of one more woman, *une femme de plus*, which is the seducer's lot. And because his goal is other than a simple object, he risks missing it in a "premature triumph."

> What then is our weakness! What is the power of circumstances if I myself, forgetting my projects, risked losing, by a premature triumph, the charm of a protracted battle and the details of a painful defeat! If, seduced by a young man's lust, I thought for a moment of letting Mme de Tourvel's conqueror, for the wages of his labor, be paid only with the insipid advantage of having had one more woman [*une femme de plus*]! Oh! let her submit, but first let her do battle; may she be too weak to win but strong enough to resist; let her savor slowly the feeling of weakness and be constrained to admit defeat. Only the lowly poacher kills the stag taken by surprise in its hiding place; the real hunter must bring him to bay. This project is sublime, is it not [*ce projet est sublime, n'est-ce pas*]? [P. 50]

As a double and therefore deferred seduction, Valmont's project is to put an end to seduction, both a term and an apotheosis. Successful, Valmont would have found a way to continue having "one more woman" even as he brings the series to a close.

It is, however, not only Valmont's duplicity which is masked by the structure of circularity. Merteuil is no less engaged in a movement between two destination points. We noted above that letter 20, which contains the contract, gets somewhat lost in a crosscurrent of Valmont's letters about Tourvel. This confusion, which the editors vainly try to sort out, may be easily overlooked by a too-circular reading. If we return now to the terms of this proposal, we find that it cannot be read simply—another reason, perhaps, that Valmont delays so long before replying. In effect, Merteuil proposes the contract as a means of putting off Valmont's request that he be allowed to "recover those moments when we knew how to attract happiness without tying it down

with the help of illusions" (p. 34), to return, in other words, to
the state of their first liaison. Merteuil's response is the contract,
which she introduces in these terms:

> It is not that I refuse permanently, but I am deferring [*je diffère*] and I
> am right. I might otherwise inject some vanity into our meeting
> and, once the game has begun, one no longer knows where [or
> when] to stop [*on ne sait plus où l'on s'arrête*]. . . . To avoid this risk,
> here are my conditions: As soon as you have had your beautiful,
> pious woman. . . . [P. 42]

In this preamble to the contract, Merteuil signals that Valmont's
desire to return to some preillusory domain of pleasure, to an
immediate, rather than a detoured, gratification, must itself be
postponed or risk becoming lost in the game of not knowing
where one stops and the other begins in a continual adjournment
of arrival. Thus, the contract which puts an end (both limit and
goal) to Valmont's seduction of Tourvel is, on the other hand, a
contract to defer that end with Merteuil. It can only offer the
illusion of some end and therefore of some return to an immediate, original correspondence. Valmont makes the mistake
of not reading this interval in Merteuil's letter and he thus will
attempt to shortcut the distance back to the marquise.

I do not mean that Valmont fails to read the letters Merteuil
addresses to him in a simple sense. Rather, what he neglects to
read, until too late, is that deviation which engages these letters
and which confuses the opposition between a direct course and a
circuitous one. Unlike Valmont's, Merteuil's dual correspondence cannot be sorted out between two addresses and distributed according to two notions inscribed alternatively. She
writes only six letters outside her exchange with the vicomte.
When compared with Valmont's total of nineteen letters to other
correspondents, the difference is the excess of the thirteen letters
he sends to Tourvel. Merteuil's letters are already letters to
another and if he misreads them then, as we have seen, it is in
part the better to ignore his own disjunction and that loss of a
singular identity which it is his project to reappropriate.

There are several different paths one could follow which would
discover traces of Merteuil's double address. Let us, however, go
at least part of the way she herself describes in letter 81, that

history of her duplicity. Note first of all that this self-portrait is prompted by Valmont's skeptical opinion of Merteuil's ability to survive her attack on Prévan. He fears she is being imprudent in taking on such a formidable project. This warning, therefore, complements Merteuil's earlier caution to Valmont that, by entering into a correspondence with Tourvel, he was proceeding too prudently and thereby risked losing his way. When Merteuil replies to this warning it is to assure him that she has no need of his prudence in order to keep on course toward the goal of seducing Prévan.

> But that you could think that I need your prudence, that I would go astray by not deferring to your opinions [*que je m'égarerais en ne déférant pas à vos avis*], that I should sacrifice a pleasure, a fantasy, to them! In truth, Vicomte, that is to take too much pride in the confidence that I have consented to have in you! [P. 172].

It goes without saying, however, that the letter in which Merteuil describes her own prudence, the trained faculty for keeping herself on course, risks going astray.

Merteuil's project, in a limited sense, is to "submit" to Prévan's advances while nevertheless defeating his intent to discredit her virtue publicly. Her aim, therefore, is to "have" Prévan in both the sexual sense and the sense of a dupe. "As for Prevan," writes Merteuil at the end of this letter, "I want to have him and I will have him; he wants to talk and he will say nothing about it [*je veux l'avoir et je l'aurai; il veut le dire et il ne le dira pas*]" (p. 181). In a larger sense, Merteuil's project is to have the other without giving up anything herself, to possess outside of an exchange in the public or symbolic register. It is only outside that register that she can have her own pleasure without becoming lost in the meaning which sustains public exchange, the meaning of the seducer's triumph and the woman's humiliation.[11] In this sense, then, Merteuil's is also a sublime project, for, like Valmont's, it would defeat the end of seduction.

This project, nevertheless, must engage in exchange with men and thus with the seducer's meaning. Merteuil has done a long apprenticeship in preparation for Prévan, who is only the most recent in the series of men she has known. If we retrace this series to its assigned beginning in letter 81, we find that it is precisely a certain knowledge, or *savoir*, that Merteuil wants to have. It is a knowledge of the man but one which no man can have. What Merteuil wants (to have/to know—*avoir/savoir*) is her own *jouissance*, but from a position which already denies that need to have and to know. It is in these terms that Merteuil describes her first "adventure":

> Like all young girls, I was seeking to figure out love and its plea-sures, but . . . I had only vague ideas that I could not pin down. Even nature, who has since given me nothing to complain about, had as yet provided no clue, as if she were working in silence to perfect her work. Only my head was excited. I had no wish for pleasure, I simply wanted to know [*je voulais savoir*].[12] The desire to learn suggested the means.
>
> I felt that the only man with whom I could speak about this subject without compromising myself was my confessor. I decided right away what to do. Overcoming my embarrassment and boast-ing of a sin which I had not committed, I accused myself of having done *everything that women do* [*tout ce que font les femmes*; in italics in original]. That was the expression I used, but in saying this I actually did not know what it was I was saying. My wish was neither altogether disappointed nor entirely fulfilled [*ni tout à fait trompé, ni entièrement rempli*]. The fear of betraying myself kept me from saying any more. But, as the good father berated me for such a great evil [*mal*], I concluded that the pleasure must be extreme. Thus after the desire to know it followed the desire to taste it. [P. 176]

This passage describes the beginning of Merteuil's project to have (to know) her own pleasure with a man's complicity but without his knowledge, to have what the man has/knows with-out exchange. Note first of all that the lack of a sign from her body of its own pleasure in itself is what must be supplied by a sign from some other place. That place will be the confessional, the scene of a particular kind of exchange which is situated in the margins of social discourse. It is thus a space within which Merteuil can strike a compromise with that discourse—in order to learn what she needs to know—without at the same time compromising herself. The confessional is also a sublime place since it provides access to the perfection Merteuil has yet to achieve, that is, to the perfect man, who, in Merteuil's terms, is one who gives her what she wants to have but says nothing about the exchange.

In this space, Merteuil confesses to "everything that women do." The "everything," however, is precisely what is lacking, what nature has failed to signify to her and in her and which thus can only be signified from some point beyond her own power to signify herself as an "everything," that is, as a finished woman. The lack is both confessed and denied, acknowledged and hidden, by the same expression which disguises the demand for the other's knowledge behind the sign of "everything." The phrase, one could say, both makes a demand and fills it, or rather makes no demand in order to disguise the demand it is making: "The fear of betraying myself," writes Merteuil, "kept me from saying any more." This closure of the demand for something else outside her limited nature is what keeps it from being closed off in a simple answer. Rather, like the question, the good Father's response defers the knowledge of pleasure through another sign: "evil" [*le mal*] (*"le mâle"*?). Merteuil is left wanting, her wish, as she writes, "neither altogether disappointed nor entirely fulfilled."

It is in this formulation of a "neither . . . nor" of Merteuil's desire to know/to have (*savoir/s'avoir*—to know/to have oneself) that we can read the double address to Valmont. In that other confessional space of letter 81, Merteuil again exposes—with less embarrassment and in more detail, to be sure—"everything that women do." As in the initial scene, however, a total *savoir* is deferred. Something remains still outside the closed circle of the self-portrait or the confession, a remainder that leaves the desire for self-possession neither completely thwarted nor totally satisfied. The deferred remainder, that which contradicts the closing off of "everything" and sends Merteuil off course, of course, is the letter.

"These precautions," writes Merteuil of her prudent procedures, "and those of never writing, never giving up [*livrer*, also to deliver] any proof of my defeat, might appear excessive but have never seemed to me sufficient" (p. 179). Once again, Merteuil discerns a choice between writing and not writing and derives a governing principle of her prudence. Yet, just like Valmont when he initiates his correspondence with Tourvel, she finally has no choice but to borrow the term which she excludes in principle. As a confession of "everything that women do," this passage is sundered in its address to the other and thereby, perhaps irretrievably, is sent into the wrong hands.

Merteuil, however, believes she possesses a return guarantee, an insurance that her letter will not go astray but will arrive intact and undivided at its destination. She continues:

> Having looked into my heart, I have also studied there the hearts of others. I learned that everyone guards a secret which it is important to keep hidden. . . . Like a new Delilah, I have always used my power to take this important secret by surprise. . . . It is true that since [the end of our affair] I have given up [*livré*] all my secrets to you. But you know what *interests* bind us to each other, and whether, of the two of us, it is I who should be accused of impru- dence. [Pp. 179–80]

In this allusion to the principle which sustains the secret ex- change between Merteuil and Valmont, to the guarantee of si- lence which keeps their joint project on course, the reader is also given a glimpse of the form which the rupture of that pact will have to take: a publication of each other's secrets through a detour imposed on the letter. For the intrigue to end, as we know, Merteuil need only deflect one of Valmont's letters outside its circuit (probably letter 96, which is addressed to her but which she passes on to Danceny) in order that every other letter in the collection be veered off course and delivered to another address. Thus, if the book and its secrets are delivered— *livrés*—into the hands of a reader, they arrive by not arriving, by not stopping at their destination.

Yet, for there to be a book, this not-arriving, this game of not-knowing-where-one-ends, must end somewhere, just as we have already remarked that the letters must also begin some- where. That is, so that the letters do not continue their course beyond the end of the book, another guarantee supplements the failed contracts between Valmont and Merteuil, serving to close off the circuit and to return the letter to its source. Something else protects the secret of the letter's drift. In *Les Liaisons Dangereuses*, this "something else" shows up in the space allotted to the only character who, as the fiction has it, writes from outside the several diverging circuits of correspondence, in those marginal notes on the bottom of the page. Two of the final notes, in particular, give some notion of what is at stake in this other pact of secrecy, the one the editor signs with the reader.

The first occurs as a note to the last passage we quoted from letter 81, where Merteuil comes dangerously close to exposing what she alludes to as the secret of Samson's strength.[13] The editor intervenes at the moment Merteuil reminds Valmont of their common "interests" and addresses this aside to the reader: "You will learn below, in letter 152, not M. de Valmont's secret but more or less of what sort it was. And the reader will understand that we are not able to enlighten him any more in this regard" (p. 180). Turning to letter 152, which is the last from Merteuil to Valmont before their secret war is declared, we find the passage that more or less reveals what cannot be revealed about Valmont. The gravity of the moment is hardly disguised by Merteuil's sarcasm:

> I could speak up but your life would be neither less brilliant nor less peaceful. And, to be honest, what would you have to fear? You might be obliged to leave, if, that is, they gave you enough time to get away. But can't one live as well elsewhere as here? On the whole, then, provided that the French court left you alone wherever you settled down, you would only be changing the scene of your triumphs. [P. 355]

We may ask to know the secret that Merteuil—teasingly or fearfully?—will not name and that the editor, appealing to discretion, cannot disclose. But it would be a pointless question since no one, apparently, can tell—including Merteuil, who, in spite of her threats, keeps silent to the end.[14] Had she not, then we have the editor's assurance of his own discretion in the affair, that supplementary guarantee. The contract not to deliver Valmont's secret, moreover, is one to which the readers will no doubt agree once they have some idea of the kind of offence involved. Suffice it to say that, were it to become known, the Crown itself might not leave such a crime unpunished. Valmont's transgression, it is suggested, is no less than an act of lèse-majesté, an attack on the symbol of legitimate power in a monarchy. Readers will also therefore infer, from Valmont's typical mode of attack, that his act of lèse-majesté could—if revealed—challenge the legitimacy of inherited rule. It is this hereditary destination of power which is guaranteed a straight line of descent by the editor's pact of silence with the reader.[15] In effect, the pact recognizes a danger to an order exterior to the novel, an order which comprises and structures the act of reading. It is thus in the reader's interest to keep a certain detour hidden.

The next editorial intervention on the vicomte's behalf suggests that not only will certain detours be silenced but still others will be enforced if the book is to arrive at its end: that is, quite simply, for the book to arrive, a certain letter—or letters—cannot. The note is appended to letter 154, from Mme de Volanges to Mme de Rosemonde. The former writes to announce the reception of a letter (which contains still another letter) and a certain decision she has made.

> I am sending you a letter I received from M. de Valmont, who has decided to choose me as a *confidente* and even as a mediator between him and Mme de Tourvel, for whom he included a letter in the one he sent to me. I sent back the former, which I enclosed in my reply to the latter. I am passing this letter on to you now and I think you will agree that I could not nor should not do anything that he asks of me. . . . But what will you think of his despair? First of all, must one believe it or does he simply want to deceive everyone right up to the end? [P. 358]

The signal for the note follows the word "end," at which point the editor interrupts to say, "It is because we found nothing in the rest [*la suite*] of this correspondence which could resolve this doubt that we have decided to suppress M. de Valmont's letter [*on a pris le parti de supprimer la lettre de M. de Valmont*]." As in the preceding note, the editor is here interjected as a backup system to insure nondelivery. Whereas, however, the discretion of the first note would seem to protect someone or something (M. de Valmont, the reader, the book) from a devastating revelation, this note also has the function of disclosure: a letter we learn, has been suppressed, not passed on.

Yet, no less than those other detours taken by the authors of the letters, this note can neither fully contain nor control the space of the excluded, suppressed term. Quite clearly from Mme de Volanges's description, there were two letters from Valmont, neither of which is included in the published collection. The first, which was addressed to Volanges herself, was sent on to Mme de Rosemonde, while the other, addressed to Tourvel, was returned to the sender. Yet the editor writes that he has decided to suppress "the letter from M. de Valmont." Which one? And why does the decision to suppress one letter entail suppressing as well not only the other letter but even the fact that this correspondence was double?

Modern editors of Laclos's work have agreed that the letter referred to in this note is the one which Laclos himself drafted and then crossed out in his final revision of the manuscript. It is addressed to Mme de Volanges and seems to be unfinished. The two most complete modern editions include this draft in appendix. (Curiously, however, in the Garnier edition, the signal for the note which would lead the reader to this letter in an appendix is missing!) Neither editor—Yves Le Hir for the Garnier edition; Maurice Allem for the Pléiade series—appears to wonder about the letter addressed to Mme de Tourvel, the one which Volanges says she returned unopened after reading Valmont's request to pass it on. This request, which we can read only in appendix, describes quite a different project for the vicomte.

> I know that my procedure [*démarche*] might appear strange to you. It surprises me myself. But despair seizes its means and does not calculate them. Besides, we share such an important and such a precious concern [*intérêt*] that it must set aside [*écarter*] every other consideration. Madame de Tourvel is dying, Madame de Tourvel is miserable. We must give her back life, health and happiness. That is the goal to be reached and any means which can assure or hasten the success are valid. . . . I plunged the dagger into your friend's heart but I alone can remove the knife from the wound. Only I have the means to cure her.[16]

Is the life which Valmont wants to give back to his mistress just another devious step in what is finally a deadly ruse? No one can tell.

This letter is suppressed, notes the editor, "because we found nothing in the rest [*suite*] of this correspondence which could resolve this doubt." Thus, what is suppressed is the *suite*, or continuation, of the doubt, the undecidability of Valmont's dual address to Tourvel which plunges in the knife with one hand and draws it out with the other. What is suppressed is also the suppression of the *other* letter from Valmont. We still have no clue as to why Volanges's decision to return Valmont's letter unread is reinforced and repeated by the editor.[17] Yet, given what we already suspect about the need to protect Valmont's secret, we might wonder if a similar public interest in the stable representation of power is not also at stake here. Who or what is delivered—saved—by the rerouting of Valmont's letter(s)? Who or what is given a reprieve from the general breakdown of the delivery system and allowed to arrive at a destination? While none of the letters' authors will be spared, their publication nevertheless serves to vindicate the only actor in the comedy who does not write: Prévan, the master seducer and Valmont's rival. The scene takes place one evening after the theater in the salon of the Comédie Italienne:

> So that nothing might be lacking from [Mme de Merteuil's] humiliation, it was her misfortune that M. de Prévan, who had not shown himself anywhere since his adventure, at that moment came into the small salon. As soon as they noticed him, everyone, men and women, surrounded him with their applause. He was, so to speak, carried before Mme de Merteuil by the public, which formed a circle around them. I was told that Mme de Merteuil pretended not to see or hear anything and that her expression did not change! But I am sure that is an exaggeration. In any case, this scene, which was really an ignominious one for her, lasted until her carriage was announced. As she was leaving, the scandalous booings increased. It is horrible to be related to such a woman. M. de Prévan was warmly welcomed by all of his fellow officers who were there and *no one doubts* that he will soon be reinstated to his post and rank. [P. 391]

Rehabilitated, Prévan saves more than himself. It is this theatrical moment which puts an end to the drama of the double inscription for all the remaining actors, the assembled society.[18] While a single figure—Samson redivivus— stands at the center of the public which has driven from its midst the scandal of his double, of the woman, a circle closes. No doubt remains.

Or rather no doubt would remain if only one knew for sure the reader's address. As the novel approaches its end and all the correspondence begins to swerve towards another destination, one letter gets diverted or intercepted for lack of a name on the envelope. It is Mme de Tourvel's last message, which she dictates to her attendant. But before she makes known to whom the letter should be sent, she falls unconscious again "so that [the chambermaid] failed to learn to whom it should be addressed." Once again, it is Mme de Volanges who intercepts this dubious communication before it gets out of hand.

> I was at first surprised that the letter itself was not sufficient to instruct her, but when she replied that she was afraid of making a mistake and that her mistress had nevertheless commanded her to send this letter right away, I took it upon myself to open the envelope. I found inside the message which I am sending you and which, in effect, addresses no one since it addresses so many people. It would seem, however, that it was at first to M. de Valmont that our unfortunate friend tried to write but that she yielded without realizing it to the disorder of her mind. Whatever the case may be, I decided that this letter should not be delivered to anyone. [P. 367]

In effect, Valmont seems to be only one among the many possible addressees of this letter, which is 161 in the collection. But if he is invoked, it is in several guises and by several voices, as may be seen in this sample from the French text which alternates between second person and third person address, *tutoiement* and *vouvoiement*.

> Etre cruel malfaisant [. . .] Mais qu'il est différent de lui-même [. . .] Mais quoi! c'est lui . . . O, mon aimable ami, oui, c'est toi, c'est bien toi! Quelle illusion funeste m'avait fait te méconnaître? . . . Tourne vers moi tes doux regards! . . . Dieu! c'est ce monstre encore! . . . Que pouvez-vous bien avoir à me dire? Ne m'avez-vous pas mise dans l'impossibilité de vous écouter comme de vous répondre? N'attendez plus rien de moi. Adieu, Monsieur. [Pp. 369–70]

This letter is diverted by Mme de Volanges, who has decided that it should be delivered to no one. She passes it on, nevertheless, to Mme de Rosemonde, who in turn hands it over to the editor, who, finally, includes it in the collection. Thus, for a letter which should not be turned over to anyone, Tourvel's last communication ends up addressing, in Mme de Volanges's phrase, "too many people." Curiously, therefore, this doubtful correspondence that dispenses with the singular address and disperses a multitude of senders and receivers slips through the editor's resolve, which operated, in the case of Valmont's questionable appeal, to suppress just such a persistence of doubt. There would appear to be yet another courier at work, one who defeats the editor's discreet refusal to forward misaddressed or fraudulent mail.

We have already noted two moments when Laclos, in what is assumed to be his final draft of the novel, hesitated over the place of a letter in the collection: letter 20, the contract letter, which initially followed letters 21 and 23, and Valmont's letter to Mme de Volanges, which Laclos first copied in the final manuscript and then crossed out.[19] Letter 161, which is headed "La Présidente de Tourvel to . . . ," was likewise the object of a certain indecision, since Laclos initially placed it before letter 160, the explanatory or cover letter from Mme de Volanges to Mme de Rosemonde. More puzzling, however, is the mobility of this letter in the autograph manuscript, which Le Hir reports as follows:

> We still have perhaps the first draft of one of the letters: that of Mme de Tourvel to the Vicomte de Valmont [*sic*: Le Hir makes clear in his index that it is letter 161 to which he refers], and which we here include in facsimile. In this draft, the letter was not numbered, only the initials of the correspondents are written, and it is on a separate sheet, thus making it easier to slip [*glisser*] into the desired place. These are all indications that this page was not intended for a copyist or even the publisher but was reserved for Laclos himself. [P. xviii]

Le Hir is cautious in suggesting that when Laclos made a final draft he did not recopy letter 161 but merely slipped in a first draft which was on a separate sheet among the pages of the revised manuscript. This careful description, however, cannot explain why this letter alone might have escaped a final revision nor why Laclos might have wished to preserve its mobility to the very end, its *glissement* into the text like a kind of fly sheet.

Although this account cannot tell us how and when the "desired place" of this letter, which is also to say its address, was finally decided, Le Hir does not hesitate to supply the part of that address which is missing in the published text ("La Présidente de Tourvel to . . . ") when he refers to it simply as the letter from Mme de Tourvel to Valmont. In this manner, the published work restores a slippage to its place in the text—and at the very place where the editor works to pin something down. In its definitive version, in other words, *Les Liaisons Dangereuses* reverts to an undecidable mode of address.

If there is another courier at work disseminating the loose mail which the editor will not pass on, might it not be in the guise of the publisher that he addresses us, the readers of this deviant work? Recall that the letters stop when a final note from this publisher suddenly reopens the pact of silence.

> For reasons of our own and other considerations which we shall always consider it our duty to respect, we are forced to stop here. At the present moment, we cannot pass on to the reader either the rest [*la suite*] of the adventures of Mlle de Volanges or an account of the sinister events which crowned the misfortunes or completed the punishment of Mme de Merteuil.
>
> One day perhaps we will be able to complete this work. But we cannot promise anything on this subject [*nous ne pouvons prendre aucun engagement à ce sujet*]. Even if we could, we should still think ourselves obligated to consult the taste of the public, which does not have the same reasons as we do to be interested in [*s'intéresser*] this reading. [P. 395]

This enigmatic intervention would seem, once again, to invoke a pact of silence, which, by forcing the book to a close, contains the detour before it can drift any further. Yet the last lines of the note shift the responsibility for this closure from author to reader, from those "reasons of our own" for ending the book of the opening sentence to the "reasons . . . to be interested in this reading" of the closing line—the reasons, that is, to continue reading beyond the forced ending. The reader, in other words, is being released by the author of this note from the contract negotiated earlier by the editor. This address sets aside the appeal to a common discretion and to an accord on the need for a protective veil thrown over the truth. Inserted in the place of a common interest, that which may be in danger if certain things are revealed, is a recognition of the reader's difference, the reader who "does not have the same reasons as we do to be interested in this reading." The only condition set on the continuation of this reading is the disengagement of interests—which is also, however, an acknowledgment of an implicit transaction between reader and text in the reflexive space of the verb *s'intéresser*. If, then, the author cannot promise to deliver the rest of the work, it is because, for the text to pass beyond the stopping point where a certain order is restored, readers will have to engage themselves in what still remains to be written.

NOTES

Introduction

1. *Héloise dans l'histoire et dans la légende*, pp. 293–363.

2. This debate continues unresolved. In her first chapter, Charrier summarizes many of the questions that have led historians, beginning in the mid-nineteenth century, to question the authenticity of the letters. She also advances the theory that Abelard, probably working from actual letters, reworked the correspondence to serve as an *exemplum* of a conversion. This position has had many proponents but also a number of dissenters, including, most recently, E. P. M. Dronke (see "Heloise and Marianne: Some Reconsiderations," *Romanische Forschungen* 72, nos. 3–4 [1960]: 223–56, and *Abelard and Heloise in Medieval Testimonies* [Glasgow: Univ. of Glasgow Press, 1976]). Etienne Gilson (*Heloise and Abelard*, trans. L. K. Stook [Ann Arbor: Univ. of Michigan Press, 1960], pp. 145–66) reviews the arguments of the *exemplum* theory and proposes his own refutation. It cannot, of course, be a question of deciding the issue and I agree with Paul Zumthor, who writes: "It does not matter: a fictive narration or an autobiographical confession, the text brings its own meaning engendered in that utopic space where the echos of the world resonate, a world against which the text constitutes itself by assimilating these echos" ("Abélard et Héloïse," preface to *Abélard et Héloïse : Correspondance*, trans. Paul Zumthor [Paris: Union Générale d'Editions, 1979], p. 12—my translation).

3. Paul Zumthor, "Héloise et Abélard," *Revue des Sciences humaines* 91 (July–September 1958): 316—my translation.

4. Ibid., p. 317.

5. Ibid., p. 317. Another who has suggested this coincidence, but without going any further, is Denis de Rougemont. In his history of courtly love, he writes: "Remember that the famous love of Abelard and Heloise is the first historical example of the passion we are discussing here" (*L'Amour et l'occident* [Paris: Plon, 1972], p. 161, n. 1—my translation; see as well pp. 54 and 84).

6. The legacy of the enclosure of difference within oppositional hierarchies can be traced through any one of the many privileged terms that are signaled in neologisms such as logocentrism, phonocentrism, phallocentrism, phallogocentrism, and androcentrism. As to why we might need such manifestly contrived terms, cf. J. Derrida, *De la grammatologie* (Paris: Minuit, 1967), chap. 1.

7. With the exception of Heloise's and Abelard's correspondence, all of the texts are cited in my own translation. This was necessary in some cases because a current translation either was not available or was clearly inadequate. Even where a current translation gives an excellent version for the English-speaking reader, I have preferred my own, since it is frequently to a literal nuance of the language or a repetition of certain words that I wish to draw attention.

Chapter 1

1. *The Letters of Abelard and Heloise*, trans. and ed. Betty Radice (Baltimore: Penguin, 1974), p. 66; all future references are to this edition and are included in the text. All italics are added. I have also consulted the French translation by Paul Zumthor (Paris: Union Générale d'Editions, 1979).

2. The critic D. W. Robertson, however, considers the whole situation "ridiculous," "absurd," and "ludicrous," and concludes that it never took place as recorded. See *Abelard and Heloise* (New York: Dial Press, 1972), p. 124.

3. A similar image occurs in Abelard's second letter to Heloise: "See then, my beloved, see how with the dragnets of his mercy the Lord has fished us up from the depth of this dangerous sea, and from the abyss of what a Charybdis he has saved our shipwrecked selves" (p. 147). This repetition could suggest that the passage in the *Historia*, which is inconsistent with the rest of the argument and has no corollary in Heloise's later correspondence, was interpolated by Abelard as he edited his memoirs.

4. Robertson (*Abelard and Heloise*), who remarks this same inconsistency, seizes on it as proof that Heloise never argued what Abelard attributes to her here. It would seem, however, that Mr. Robertson's own logic is flawed by this confusion of literary verisimilitude with historical fact. We will return to this point below.

5. Elizabeth Hamilton speculates that Fulbert, whose ambiguous relation to Heloise has always puzzled historians, might have had more than a parental interest in her sexual honor. See *Heloise* (Garden City, New York: Doubleday, 1967), p. 20.

6. E. P. M. Dronke, while admitting that "a detailed commentary on

the large, impersonal part of the Abelard-Heloise correspondence would require, and deserve, a book" ("Heloise and Marianne: Some Reconsiderations," *Romanische Forschungen* 72, nos. 3–4 (1960): 239), nevertheless analyzes selected moments when the directional letters seem to refer very closely to the situation of the personal letters. My own reading of the correspondence, while it diverges on some major points, still owes a great deal to Dronke's sensitive yet unflinching interpretations in this article, as well as to his more recent *Abelard and Heloise in Medieval Testimonies.*

7. Gilson, *Heloise and Abelard*, p. 167.

8. Dronke hesitates to qualify as systematic Abelard's misreading, but he notes: "His total misunderstanding of her letter is proof enough that he did not write it!" ("Heloise and Marianne," p. 235).

9. "Unico suo post Christum, unica sua in Christo." Dronke discusses this superscription as a concession to the order Abelard has established but reserves the possibility of another, still reproachful, reading. See "Heloise and Marianne," p. 238.

10. The translator adds this note: "This sentence, often mistranslated as if it refers to the present and so suggesting that Abelard has never visited nor written to her at the Paraclete, has been used as evidence that the letters are a forgery because it contradicts what Abelard says in the *Historia calamitatum* (98). But the tense (*movit*) is past, translated here as 'I was troubled,' and Heloise must be referring to his failure to help her by word before they separated and by letter after she had entered the convent." Gilson's research into the Benedictine usage of the related terms *conversio* and *conversation*—the first, conversion to the faith; the second, entrance into the monastic rule—helps clarify this passage and others where translations have tended to imply similar contradictions of the *Historia*. See Gilson, *Heloise and Abelard*, pp. 143–60.

11. Robertson, *Abelard and Heloise*, pp. 50 and 53.

12. One could even argue that Heloise is not all that inconsistent, for the final position attributed to her—and the point of departure for the development I am following in the letter—does not contradict the distinction of wedlock and virtue. Clearly she understands virtue in a sense which does not exclude—on the contrary—concubinage. The functioning distinctions throughout the argument are the pairs of oppositions husband/master, wife/mistress, and not, as one might be tempted to conclude from the classical context of her rhetoric, continence/incontinence. This latter distinction collapses wedlock and concubinage, which it recognizes as but two forms of the failure of sexual chastity. Heloise, as we have already said, makes very little case for this latter concept and invokes much more consistently the desirability of the philosophical ideal of purity.

13. In the Latin, the series ends *"vel* scorti." While Radice did not choose to translate *vel* as the conjunction introducing the superlative in a list ("or *even* whore"), it is permitted and indicated by our analysis.

14. This analysis is consistent with Dronke's interpretation of Heloise's submission to Abelard's law, his *jussio*. However, by retrieving the link to the erotic scene, where that submission is undone in its relation to the law, I am suggesting that Abelard's *jussio* continues to function as pretext.

15. The translator notes that in the Latin original the expression is *Vulcania loca*, which, she says, "illustrates how Heloise's natural manner of expressing herself is classical" (p. 117). When we come to consider Heloise's refusal of the symbols of Christian transcendence, this classical expression takes on another significance.

16. While it is left standing here, this formulation is overturned in a passage from the earlier letter, where similar terms produce a different conclusion: "While I enjoyed with you the pleasures of the flesh, many were uncertain whether I was prompted by love or lust; but now the end is proof of the beginning. I have finally denied myself every pleasure in obedience to your will, kept nothing for myself except to prove that now, even more, I am yours" (p. 117).

17. Heloise employs a similar figure in at least two other places. In the opening section of this letter, she pleads with Abelard to avoid calling up any more images of his own death: "I beg you, spare us—spare her at least, who is yours alone, by refraining from words like these. They pierce our hearts with swords of death, so that what comes before is more painful than death itself" (p. 128); also, in the transitional first paragraph of her third letter, where she reluctantly agrees to observe the limits Abelard has placed on any future exchange, she concedes that "as one nail drives out another hammered in, a new thought expels an old, when the mind is intent on other things and forced to dismiss or interrupt its recollection of the past" (p. 159).

18. *Song of Songs* 1:4–5.

19. In the *Historia calamitatum*, Abelard gives an example of his extraordinary talent for scriptural exegesis. While a student of Anselm's, he boasted to his classmates that, although he had only begun his biblical studies, he could produce as good an exposition of any text as the master. The other students challenged him with "an extremely obscure prophecy of Ezekiel" and Abelard promised his exposition for the next day. According to this account, no one really believed that, with so little training and time, he could produce anything worthwhile. The lecture came off as scheduled and was such a success that it provoked Anselm to attack him out of jealousy (pp. 63–64).

20. Abelard supposes very white teeth for his portrait of the bride, these being the only visible mark of her hidden beauty. Teeth are at the limit of the opposition exterior/interior, manifest/hidden, and thus mark the coincidence of a sign with what is signified. For this reason as well, beautiful teeth is the only term in the larger analogy between the black bride and the nun which is not symbolized—as black skin is symbolized by the black habit—but merely repeated. Abelard, it would seem, is referring to Heloise's own beautiful teeth. Note that in some accounts of the several exhumations of Heloise's remains, the recorder noted the "extreme whiteness of the teeth" which were found in the coffin (Charlotte Charrier, *Héloïse dans l'histoire et dans la légende*, p. 317). One can, of course, always speculate on whether or not such an observation was already prescribed by Abelard's appreciation of this feature.

21. Zumthor, in "Héloïse et Abélard," *Revue des Sciences humaines* 91 (July–September 1958): 313–31, analyzes the secrecy of the marriage as both a rejection of the feudal ethic, represented by Fulbert, and an attempt to maintain an effective obstacle to the union of the lovers even as that union is celebrated. This interpretation does not exclude the analysis I have undertaken of the same material, although I cannot agree that the courtly topos can render an adequate translation of the full text of Heloise's letters, an inadequacy which Zumthor only recognizes when discussing Abelard's texts.

22. Abelard describes the disruption of his effectiveness as master of schools during the period of his cohabitation with Heloise: "Now the more I was taken up with these pleasures, the less time I could give to philosophy and the less attention I paid to my school. It was utterly boring for me to have to go to the school, and equally wearisome to remain there and to spend my days on study when my nights were sleepless with love-making. As my interest and concentration flagged, my lectures lacked all inspiration and were merely repetitive; I could do no more than repeat what had been said long ago, and when inspiration did come to me, it was for writing love-songs, not the secrets of philosophy. . . . [T]he grief and sorrow and laments of my students when they realized my preoccupation, or rather, distraction of mind, are hard to realize. Few could have failed to notice something so obvious" (p. 68).

23. It is possible to see here a link between Abelard's method of reading Heloise's letters and the principles of his theology of ethics. Richard E. Weingart, in his study *The Logic of Divine Love: A Critical Analysis of the Soteriology of Peter Abailard*, identifies the concept of radical interiorization as Abelard's chief contribution to the teaching of sin, and summarizes this concept as follows: "Sin is interior; it is free,

personal, deliberate, responsible consent to some evil. In the area of ethics in general, intention is the controlling factor, for it determines the moral valuation of any action. Acts are morally indifferent and given value only through the intention of the agent. Intention, like consent, is an interior disposition of the soul perceptible to God alone. Consequently, Abailard's concept of *consensus* and *intentio* are the hallmarks of his teaching on sin and the moral life, hallmarks which manifest his unique and radical interiorization of sin" (p. 65). Commentators of the correspondence have not failed to point out the moments in Heloise's letters when she seems to be referring to what she knows of this principle. For example: "Wholly guilty though I am, I am also, as you know, wholly innocent. It is not the deed but the *intention* of the doer which makes the crime, and justice should weigh not what was done but the spirit in which it is done" (p. 115); and, "At least I can thank God for this: the tempter did not prevail on me to do wrong of my own *consent*" (p. 131).

24. This analysis of the erotic game has, of course, an almost unlimited applicability to Western literature. I discussed some of its implications for the concept of feminine modesty in "Rousseau's Politics of Visibility," *Diacritics*, Winter 1975, pp. 51–56.

25. Besides a quotation from Lucan's *Pharsalia*, this is the only other non-Christian source from which Abelard quotes in this letter. Classical letters represent that body of literature which Abelard repudiates in his conversion from philosophy to theology, for, as he suggests later on in his letter, his punishment was a sign that God "was indignant or grieved because our knowledge of letters, the talents which he had entrusted to us, were not being used to glorify his name" (p. 149). On the other hand, classical references prevail almost equally with biblical ones and references to the Church fathers in Heloise's two letters (see note 15 above).

26. This analysis of an integrated yet foreign term in the unity of the pure, self-present subject, has become familiar since Jacques Derrida's *De la grammatologie* (Paris: Minuit, 1967) and its exposition of the dynamic of "ce dangereux supplément" throughout the text of Rousseau. One of the threads with which that text embroiders on the supplement is the danger of auto-eroticism, which introduces Rousseau to the scandal whereby "nothing seems more natural than this destruction of nature" (p. 216).

27. This passage, however, occurs in connection with Abelard's account of his forced flight from the Paraclete after his presence there provoked a scandal: "My detractors, with their usual perverseness, had the effrontery to accuse me of doing what divine charity prompted

because I was still a slave to the pleasures of carnal desire and could rarely or never bear the absence of the woman I had once loved" (p. 98). This "perverse" accusation undoes the simple equation of sexual desire with genital potency on which Abelard grounds his renunciation, so that his enslavement remains ambiguously mortgaged to that other master.

Chapter 2

1. See Leo Spitzer, "Les *Lettres portugaises*," *Romanische Forschungen* 65, nos. 1–2 (1953): 94–135; and E. P. M. Dronke "Heloise and Marianne," *Romanische Forschungen* 72, nos. 3–4 (1960): 223–56.

2. "On Feminine Sexuality," vol. 21 of *The Standard Edition of the Complete Psychological Works*.

3. *The Origins of Psychoanalysis: Sigmund Freud's Letters to Wilhelm Fliess*, p. 216.

4. *Letters to Fliess*, p. 215. Jean Laplanche and J. -B. Pontalis have shown, however, in a careful reading of Freud's later works, that the notion of the "original fantasy" retained a significant link to the alternative theory of the reality of a seduction. They write: "When, taking up the official view of Freud himself, the historians of psychoanalysis tell us that the abandonment of the theory of seduction, in face of evidence to the contrary, cleared the path for the discovery of infantile sexuality, they simplify an evolution which was much more ambiguous" ("Fantasme originaire, fantasmes des origines, origine du fantasme," in *Les Temps modernes* 215 [April 1964]: 1844). As it is not my purpose here to rewrite the official history of psychoanalysis, but only to remark how a woman's discourse gets lost in the progress of scientific discovery, I have simplified in terms which are very close to those that Laplanche and Pontalis remark.

5. For a more detailed reading of this same development in the theory of hysteria, see Catherine Clément's essay "La Coupable" in *La Jeune née*, coauthored with Hélène Cixous (Paris: Union Générale d'Éditions, 1975).

6. *Letters to Fliess*, introduction by Steven Marcus, pp. 27ff.

7. *Letters to Fliess*, pp. 267–68.

8. Luce Irigaray, "La Tache aveugle d'un vieux rêve de symétrie," in *Speculum de l'autre femme*. See as well "Retour sur la théorie psychanalytique" in *Ce Sexe qui n'en est pas un* (Paris: Minuit, 1977).

9. See Josette Féral, "Antigone or *The Irony of the Tribe*," *Diacritics*, Fall 1978, pp. 2–14.

10. Clément, "La Coupable," p. 104.

11. "General Remarks on Hysterical Attacks," in *Dora: An Analysis of a Case of Hysteria*, p. 157.

12. *Dora*, pp. 26–27.

13. Herr K. was Dora's father's closest associate while Frau K. was his mistress. Her hysteria was thus structured not only on a desire for the father but also a desire like the father's.

14. *Studies on Hysteria*, p. 17; my italics.

15. Ernest Jones, *The Life and Work of Sigmund Freud*, 1:223–26.

16. *Studies on Hysteria*, p. 305.

17. Clément, "La Coupable," p. 80.

18. *Dora*, p. 140.

19. This is, in a sense, Philip Rieff's conclusion when he writes in his introduction to the case history: "Freud's insight was superior to Dora's. Hers had not helped her win more than pyrrhic victories over life. . . . Her own understanding of life had in no way given her any power to change it; precisely that power to change life was Freud's test of truth. His truth was, therefore, superior to Dora's. But the mystery of character never submits entirely, even to the greatest masters. There are fresh reserves of motive which, unexamined, will not yield to reason, however therapeutic might be the experience of yielding" (pp. 11–12).

20. Clément, "La Coupable," p. 288.

21. One might consider the difference with another of Freud's famous cases, Serguei P., the Wolf Man, who, though equally reluctant to give up his illness, was a very active painter throughout his life and eventually wrote his memoirs. Like the Wolf Man case, the case of Dora has recently come under scrutiny again from both analysts and other critical readers, and my remarks here are not meant to pose any definitive reinterpretation of this material, which is very rich. Clément's and Cixous's *La Jeune née*, part of which stages, in dialogue form, a disagreement about the significance of Dora's case, discusses some other implications of the hysterical model. Also, a chapter in Jane Gallop's *Feminism and Psychoanalysis* (New York: MacMillan Co., forthcoming) submits the case to a thorough reexamination whose conclusions take one far beyond the suggestions I have made here to explain the "failure" of the analysis.

22. This epistolary account of a woman's seduction and betrayal has had an eventful critical history which I have discussed in "Writing Like a Woman," in *Women and Language in Literature and Society*, ed. Sally McConnell-Ginet, Ruth Borker, and Nelly Furman (New York: Praeger, 1980).

23. *Les Lettres portugaises*, eds. F. Deloffre and J. Rougeot (Paris: Garnier, 1962), p. 39; all future references are to this edition and are

included in the text. The current English translation by Donald E. Ericson, which follows a discredited edition of the text, is reprinted in *The Three Marias: New Portuguese Letters* (New York: Doubleday, 1974).

24. Deloffre's and Rougeot's glossary of classical love vocabulary has this entry for *mouvement*: "This word . . . always applies to the spontaneous ecstasies, emotions or feelings which escape the control of the will and even consciousness" (p. 265).

25. Louise Horowitz, *Love and Language: A Study of the Classical French Moralist Writers*, pp. 142–43.

Chapter 3

1. One of the best among recent histories of the genre is English Showalter's *The Evolution of the French Novel, 1641–1782* (Princeton: Princeton University Press, 1972).

2. The impersonal narrator is, of course, conventional in both the epic and the courtly romances. But neither of these fictional modes pretends to the plausibility of Mme de Lafayette's novel. For other significant distinctions between this novel and its predecessor modes, cf. Sylvère Lotringer, "La Structuration romanesque," *Critique* 26, no. 277 (June 1970).

3. Jean Fabre, *L'Art de l'analyse dans la Princesse de Clèves*, p. 70.

4. Mme de Lafayette, *Romans et nouvelles* (Paris: Garnier, 1961), p. 247; all future references are to this edition and are included in the text. All italics are added.

5. The Sadian father, whose education of his daughters takes place in the boudoir, is thus perhaps the most direct heir of Mme de Chartres's educational philosophy insofar as he reclaims this pedagogical prerogative from hired tutors. Cf. Jane Gallop, "Impertinent Questions: Irigaray, Sade, Lacan," *Sub-Stance*, no. 26 (1980): 57–67.

6. Lotringer bases his analysis of the novel in part on this contamination or complicity of virtue and libertinism which allows the court to function cohesively in a context of false difference.

7. Nancy Mitford's translation (New York: Penguin, 1978) sacrifices this ambiguity rather freely: "She felt no qualms; it never even occurred to her that she was perhaps giving her daughter to somebody whom she could not love" (p. 48).

8. I have not tried to render my translation any less ambiguous than the original, where the antecedents of "she" and "her" in the last clause are indeterminate. At several other places in the text, Mme de Chartres and her daughter likewise become grammatically interchangeable.

9. Serge Leclaire has designated this process in the title of a collection of case studies, each of which illustrates a different relation to this

ritual execution: *On tue un enfant* (Paris: Seuil, 1975). In each case, the analysis insists on the dual character of the execution, which is "as imperative as it is impossible to accomplish" (pp. 25–26): imperative, because it is a mad destiny which awaits anyone who chooses to remain on this side of desire; impossible, because the representation of the child is unconscious and thus indelible, at the very origin of every other representation of the subject. But it is, once again, this notion of a single source to which all other elaborations of the self ultimately return that must be contested even as one contests the despotism of absolute power. "What must be put to death are the constructions and fantasies which claim to account for our filiation in a univocal fashion or, more precisely, that focalize in a single point of origin the source of the forces that move us. We are truly, at the same time, 'children of God' . . . and deicidal" (pp. 56–57).

10. At an earlier moment, when Mme de Clèves first contemplates confessing to her husband, it is once again the force of the name which stops her: "She was on the point of telling him of the rumor that M. de Nemours was in love with her, but she did not have the force to name him" (p. 296).

11. Michel Butor, "Sur *La Princesse de Clèves*," in *Répertoire* (Paris: Minuit, 1960), pp. 76–77.

12. This repetition is also signaled in the discourse of each character: Mme de Chartres's "I am no longer in a position to rely on your sincerity" (p. 227) is echoed when Clèves says, "I am no longer in a position to reproach you" (p. 374).

Chapter 4

1. Charlotte Charrier, *Héloïse dans l'histoire et dans la légende*, p. 466.

2. Vol. 2 of *Oeuvres complètes*, ed. Henri Coulet and Bernard Guyon, (Paris: Pléïade, 1964), n. 1, pp. 1336–38. All future references are to this edition and are in the text. All italics are added.

3. Letter to M.-M. Rey, *Correspondance complète de Jean-Jacques Rousseau*, vol. 7, letter 1037.

4. Ibid.

5. As I hope will become clear, I am not suggesting that this danger is that of any romantic fiction in the hands of an Emma Bovary-style reader. I concur, rather, with Paul de Man, who writes: "The evil of the letters can be too easily attributed to their literary mediation, to the desire they convey in the guise of fictions. . . . The danger of reading is a far-reaching and invidious threat that no conversion, however radical, could ever hope to remove" (*Allegories of Reading: Figural Language in*

Rousseau, Nietzsche, Rilke and Proust [New Haven: Yale University Press, 1979], pp. 194–95).

6. For de Man, the "neo-medieval title" invites us to regard the novel as a "figural abstraction" which, rather than as an analogy to some fixed referent, he considers in the mode of deconstructive allegory (*Allegories of Reading*, p. 189).

7. "Héloïse et Abélard," pp. 321–22.

8. Vol. 3 of *Oeuvres complètes*, ed. Robert Derathé, p. 243; all references are to this edition and are included in the text.

9. Tony Tanner discerns the same crisis in the novel: "The Word of the father is here in a very imperiled condition. His family name and the titles are becoming meaningless, based on functions, distinctions, and differences that were ceasing to exist" (*Adultery in the Novel: Contract and Transgression* [Baltimore: Johns Hopkins University Press, 1979], p. 138). Tanner also reminds us that, through their subjugation to Berne, the nobility of the Vaud region had been excluded from public office and were thus noble in name only (p. 142).

10. At length, but not *in toto*. The most significant portion of what I have omitted concerns the mother's reaction to this scene. One may, to be sure, read that for oneself.

11. "Preux" is from the Latin *prodesse*—"to be useful."

12. Of course, ambiguity marks the lover's name at another level since "Saint-Preux" is adopted as a pseudonym. In addition, we have here another way of thinking about this character's "effeminacy," which has been remarked by several critics, for example, Carol Blum, who writes of Saint-Preux's "oddly womanish, hysterical nature" ("*La Nouvelle Héloïse*: An Act in the Life of Jean-Jacques Rousseau," *L'Esprit Créateur* 9 [Fall 1969]: p. 203).

13. Since this doubleness will be played out as well in the naming of the garden, the question of whose garden it is cannot have a simple answer. Tanner (*Adultery in the Novel*) inadvertently signals this undecidability with a slip on p. 158: "We should note that it is very much *Claire's* garden, her creation as well as her fantasy"; this is corrected on p. 160 when he writes: "It is, I said, very much *Julie's* garden" (my italics). It is interesting that when attempting to assign exclusive ownership of the garden, one gets it wrong. This could, of course, point to the inseparability of the cousins, a notion which Tanner analyzes at some length.

14. Tanner, who also remarks on the importance of the water in the garden, thus falls into another mistake (see n. 12) when he traces it back to a single source: " . . . the water (which, note, *all* comes from a gush of water at a place that was made by the father—once again he is the source)" (*Adultery in the Novel*, pp. 156–57; my italics).

15. Although more accurately Julie "throws herself after [her son]," the same letter reporting the incident to Saint-Preux, from Fanchon Anet, also refers to the accident as "the fall" (pp. 702–703).

16. I refer to the notion of repetition through substitution which Godelieve Mercken-Spaas makes use of in her analysis of the novel, *"La Nouvelle Héloïse:* La Répétition à la deuxième puissance," (*Studies in Eighteenth-Century Culture*, vol. 5, ed. Ronald C. Rosbottom [Madison: University of Wisconsin Press, 1976], pp. 203–213) and which she has in turn borrowed from Gilles Deleuze. Mercken-Spaas, however, does not discuss the structure of the repetition in Julie's two falls.

17. Jean-Jacques Rousseau, *Les Confessions*, vol. 1 of *Oeuvres complètes*, ed. Bernard Gagnebin and Marcel Raymond, p. 22; all future references are to this edition and are included in the text.

Chapter 5

1. Our analysis of the letter's detour sets out from a number of points with which Jacques Derrida marks his traversal of another letter-fiction, Poe's "Purloined Letter," in "Le Facteur de la vérité" (translated as "The Purveyor of Truth" by Willis Domingo, James Hulbert, Moshe Ron, and M.-R. Logan in *Yale French Studies*, no. 52 [1975]): 31–113. Or rather, instead of points, it is a series of bifurcations that have led us from the context of Derrida's essay to that of Laclos's novel and several of the critical interpretations it has called up. This transmittal, therefore, will not have occurred without some loss along the way as well as some doubling back, and if we cite here a passage from that essay, it is perhaps as a reminder that work on the letter, including our own, continues: "The divisibility of the letter . . . is what puts in jeopardy and leads astray, with no guarantee of return, the remnant of anything whatever: a letter does *not always* arrive at its destination, and since this belongs to its structure, it can be said that it never really arrives there, that when it arrives, its possibly-not-arriving torments it with an internal divergence" (p. 107). This essay has recently been reedited and, along with several other texts concerned with the network of letters and destination, included in *La Carte postale* (Paris: Aubier-Flammarion, 1980).

2. Saint-Preux writes: "I hope that I would never forget myself to the point of speaking to you of that which you should not hear" (p. 31).

3. *Les Liaisons dangereuses*, ed. Yves Le Hir (Paris: Garnier, 1961), p. 27. All future references included in the text will be to this edition. Notes will indicate any reference to the edition of the text included in *Les Oeuvres complètes*, ed. Maurice Allem (Paris: Bibliothèque de la Pléïade, 1951). All italics are added.

4. There is no such pure outside for Rousseau's novel either, of course. The warning in the preface, as we recall, considerably extends the region of the detour beyond the letter and beyond the book. "She who, in spite of this title, dares to read a single page is lost. But let her not impute her loss to this book: the harm was *already* done" (p. 6). Likewise, our reading of the aqueduct anecdote suggests that the sexual oppositions of the novel are more devious than they appear.

5. Tzvetan Todorov, *Littérature et signification*, p. 43.

6. Merteuil's repeated reference to Valmont's invention (for example, "You simply do not have the genius of your position. You only know what you have learned and you invent nothing" [p. 248], and, "In truth, Vicomte, you are not inventive" [p. 267]) invites a comparison with Shoshana Felman's recent analysis of Don Juan's performative acts in *Le Scandale du corps parlant* (Paris: Seuil, 1980). It is interesting to note, however, that such a comparison would have to leave out of account the doubled *parole* of the *Liaisons Dangereuses*. The success of Don Juan's sui-referential performance depends finally on the singularity of the self-reference. The Don's victims can be victimized precisely because they choose to operate within the objective reference of constative discourse rather than the self-reference of his performative discourse. His enterprise, in other words, relies on this difference by which he is the most successful performer because he is the only performer. Valmont, however, from the beginning must share the stage with Merteuil, to whom he writes, in his first letter to her, "You are following me at an equal pace at least and since, having separated for the good of the world, we have both been preaching the faith, it seems to me that in this mission of love, you have made more converts than I" (p. 12).

7. This note reads: "This letter, which responds to letter 15, crossed with letters 17 and 18. We preferred to place it after so that the reader might know Valmont's situation when he received it" (p. 41). The numbers 17 and 18 would seem to correspond to a first ordering of the letters and to indicate letters 21 and 23 in the final version, both of which are from Valmont to Merteuil. Thus the letter in question—letter 20—is finally placed not after but before these others. The inclusion of this note (which the Pléïade edition moves to the appendix) serves only, therefore, to distract and disorient the reader.

8. Aram Vartanian, "The Marquise de Merteuil: A Case of Mistaken Identity," *L'Esprit Créateur*, 3 (Winter 1963), p. 179.

9. Georges Daniel, *Fatalité du secret, fatalité du bavardage au XVIIIe siècle: Mme de Merteuil, Le Neveu de Rameau*, p. 18.

10. Valmont's movement between Merteuil and Tourvel, between, therefore, the origin of an identity and its dispersion in passion, is to be compared to the Princess de Clèves's hesitation between mother (hus-

band) and lover. The two identities in question define each other perfectly: the princess as unattainable woman and Valmont as irresistible seducer.

11. An analysis of the complicity between the seducer's scandal and the public's virtue would find a model in this articulation of Mme de Volanges's *inconsistency*: "I do not deny that I receive M. de Valmont and that he is received everywhere. It is one more inconsistency to add to the thousand others that govern society. You know, as I do, that one spends one's life noticing them, complaining about them, and giving into them" (p. 65). This analysis has been carried out most perceptively by Sylvère Lotringer in "Vice de forme" (*Critique* 27, no. 286 [March 1971]) which relies on a previous discussion of similar structures in *The Princess de Clèves* ("La Structuration romanesque" [*Critique* 26, no. 277 (June 1970)]). We will discuss below another representation of this complicity—as well as Mme de Volanges's role as its key representative.

12. Baudelaire, who for more than ten years referred off and on to a projected critical study of *Les Liaisons Dangereuses*, made sparse notes on the novel which frequently consisted merely in quotations. A part of this passage is cited there as follows: "Je ne désirais pas de jouir, je *voulais* SAVOIR" (*Oeuvres complètes* de Laclos, ed. Maurice Allem [Paris: Pléïade, 1951], p. 720).

13. The companion piece to this letter is letter 85, in which Merteuil recounts her Delilah-like triumph over Prévan. It is important to note, however, that this modern Samson is not defeated by the sort of blackmail which Merteuil claims she employs in such cases. Rather, the secret of Prévan's strength, and therefore his weakness, is precisely that which is not hidden at all: his proud reputation as a seducer.

14. When Merteuil does retaliate, she delivers not this secret but that of Valmont's seduction of Cécile and betrayal of Danceny. This substitution could suggest, however, that it is a similar transgression that must be silenced.

15. Thus, the *Liaisons Dangereuses*, at its most secret level, rejoins *Julie* in its preoccupation with the detour of the father's legitimacy.

16. Quoted from the Pléïade edition, pp. 830–31.

17. Another reader has suggested several possible explanations; see Ronald Rosbottom, *Choderlos de Laclos* (Boston: Twayne, 1978), p. 106.

18. Nancy K. Miller describes Merteuil's humiliation—and the end of the novel—as the "death of the Other [that] restores men to each other" in her article, "The Exquisite Cadavers: Women in Eighteenth-Century Fiction," *Diacritics*, Winter 1975, pp. 42–43.

19. For a list of the other reorderings, see Le Hir, pp. xvii–xviii or Allem, p. xxv.

BIBLIOGRAPHY

Primary Texts

Abelard, Peter. *Petri Abelardi Opera*. 2 vols. Edited by V. Cousin. Paris: 1849 and 1859.

[Guilleragues.] *Les Lettres Portugaises*. Edited by F. Deloffre and J. Rougeot. Paris: Garnier, 1962.

Laclos, Choderlos de. *Les Liaisons dangereuses*. Edited by Yves Le Hir. Paris: Garnier, 1961.

———. *Oeuvres complètes*. Edited by Maurice Allem. Paris: Bibliothèque de la Pléïade, 1951.

Lafayette, Mme de. *Romans et nouvelles*. Edited by Emile Magne. Paris: Garnier, 1961.

Rousseau, Jean-Jacques. *Correspondance complète*. Edited by R. A. Leigh. Geneva: Institut et Musée Voltaire; Madison: University of Wisconsin Press, 1969.

———. *Oeuvres complètes*. 4 vols. Edited by Bernard Gagnebin and Marcel Raymond. Paris: Bibliothèque de la Pléïade, 1959–69.

Translations Consulted

Abélard et Héloïse: Correspondance. Translated by Paul Zumthor. Paris: Union Générale d'Editions, 1979.

The Letters of Abelard and Heloise. Translated by Betty Radice. Baltimore: Penguin, 1974.

Les Liaisons Dangereuses. Translated by P. W. K. Stone. New York: Penguin, 1961.

The Princesse de Clèves. Translated by Nancy Mitford. New York: Penguin, 1978.

The Portuguese Letters. Translated by Donald E. Ericson. In *The Three Marias: New Portuguese Letters*. New York: Doubleday, 1974.

Critical Works Cited

Abraham, Nicolas. *L'Ecorce et le noyau*. Paris: Aubier-Flammarion, 1978.

Blum, Carol. "*La Nouvelle Héloïse*: An Act in the Life of Jean-Jacques Rousseau." *L'Esprit Créateur*, 9 (Fall 1969): 198–206.

Butor, Michel. "Sur *La Princesse de Clèves*." In *Répertoire*. Paris: Minuit, 1960.

Charrier, Charlotte. *Héloïse dans l'histoire et dans la légende*. Geneva: Slatkine Reprints, 1977.

Clément, Catherine, and Cixous, Hélène. *La Jeune née*. Paris: Union Générale d'Editions, 1975.

Daniel, Georges. *Fatalité du secret, fatalité du bavardage au XVIIIe siècle: Mme de Merteuil, Le Neveu de Rameau*. Paris: Nizet, 1966.

de Man, Paul. *Allegories of Reading: Figural Language in Rousseau, Nietzsche, Rilke and Proust*. New Haven: Yale University Press, 1979.

Derrida, Jacques. *La Carte postale: De Socrate à Freud et au-delà*. Paris: Aubier-Flammarion, 1980.

———. "Fors." Translated by Barbara Johnson. *The Georgia Review*, Spring 1977, pp. 64–116.

———. *De la grammatologie*. Paris: Minuit, 1967.

———. "The Purveyor of Truth." Translated by W. Domingo, J. Hulbert, M. Ron, and M.-R. Logan. *Yale French Studies* 52 (1975).

Dronke, E. P. M. *Abelard and Heloise in Medieval Testimonies*. Glasgow: University of Glasgow Press, 1976.

———. "Heloise and Marianne: Some Reconsiderations." *Romanische Forschungen* 72, nos. 3–4 (1960): 223–56.

Fabre, Jean. *L'Art de l'analyse dans la Princesse de Clèves*. Paris: Ophrys, 1970.

Felman, Shoshana. *Le Scandale du corps parlant: Don Juan avec Austin ou la séduction en deux langues*. Paris: Seuil, 1980.

Féral, Josette. "Antigone or *The Irony of the Tribe*." *Diacritics*, Fall 1978, pp. 2–14.

Freud, Sigmund. *Dora: An Analysis of a Case of Hysteria*. Edited by Philip Reiff. New York: Collier, 1963.

———. "On Feminine Sexuality." *The Standard Edition of the Complete Psychological Works*. Vol. 21. London: Hogarth Press, 1955.

———. "General Remarks on Hysterical Attacks." In *Dora*. Edited by Philip Reiff. New York: Collier, 1963.

———. *The Origins of Psychoanalysis: Sigmund Freud's Letters to Wilhelm Fliess*. Translated by Eric Mosbacher and James Strachey. New York: Basic Books, 1954.

———. and Breuer, Joseph. *Studies on Hysteria*. *The Standard Edition of the Complete Psychological Works*. Vol. 2. London: Hogarth Press, 1955.

Gallop, Jane. "Impertinent Questions: Irigaray, Sade, Lacan." *SubStance* 26 (1980): 57–67.

Gilson, Etienne. *Heloise and Abelard*. Translated by L. K. Stook. Ann Arbor: University of Michigan Press, 1960.

Hamilton, Elizabeth. *Heloise*. Garden City, New York: Doubleday, 1967.

Horowitz, Louise. *Love and Language: A Study of the Classical French Moralist Writers*. Columbus: The Ohio State University Press, 1977.

Irigaray, Luce. *Ce Sexe qui n'en est pas un*. Paris: Minuit, 1977.

———. *Speculum de l'autre femme*. Paris: Minuit, 1974.

Jones, Ernest. *The Life and Work of Sigmund Freud*. New York: Basic Books, 1953.

Kamuf, Peggy. "Rousseau's Politics of Visibility." *Diacritics*, Winter 1975, pp. 51–56.

———. "Writing Like a Woman." In *Women and Language in Literature and Society*. Edited by Sally McConnell-Ginet, Ruth Borker, and Nelly Furman. New York: Praeger, 1980.

Laplanche, Jean, and Pontalis, J.-B. "Fantasme originaire, fantasmes des origines, origine du fantasme." *Les Temps modernes* 215 (April 1964): 1833–68.

Leclaire, Serge. *On tue un enfant*. Paris: Seuil, 1975.

Lotringer, Sylvère. "La Structuration romanesque." *Critique* 26, no. 277 (June 1970): 498–529.

———. "Vice de forme." *Critique* 27, no. 286 (March 1971): 195–209.

Mercken-Spaas, Godelieve. "*La Nouvelle Héloïse*: La Répétition à la deuxième puissance." In *Studies in Eighteenth-Century Culture*. Vol. 5. Edited by Ronald C. Rosbottom. Madison: University of Wisconsin Press, 1976.

Miller, Nancy K. "The Exquisite Cadavers: Woman in Eighteenth-Century Fiction." *Diacritics*, Winter 1975, pp. 37–43.

Robertson, D. W. *Abelard and Heloise*. New York: Dial Press, 1972.

Rosbottom, Ronald. *Choderlos de Laclos*. Boston: Twayne, 1978.

Rougemont, Denis de. *L'Amour et l'occident*. Paris: Plon, 1972.

Showalter, English. *The Evolution of the French Novel, 1641–1782*. Princeton: Princeton University Press, 1972.

Spitzer, Leo. "Les *Lettres portugaises*." *Romanische Forschungen* 65, nos. 1–2 (1953): 94–135.

Tanner, Tony. *Adultery in the Novel: Contract and Transgression*. Baltimore: The Johns Hopkins University Press, 1979.

Todorov, Tzvetan. *Littérature et signification*. Paris: Gallimard, 1968.

Vartanian, Aram. "The Marquise de Merteuil: A Case of Mistaken Identity." *L'Esprit Créateur* 3, no. 4 (Winter 1963): 172–80.

Weingart, Richard E. *The Logic of Divine Love: A Critical Analysis of the Soteriology of Peter Abailard*. Oxford: Clarendon Press, 1970.

Zumthor, Paul. "Héloïse et Abélard." *Revue des Sciences humaines* 91 (July–September 1968): 313–31.

INDEX